Educational Leadership and Hannah Arendt

The relationship between education and democratic development has been a growing theme in debates focused upon public education, but there has been little work that has directly related educational leadership to wider issues of freedom, politics and practice. Engaging with ELMA through the work of Hannah Arendt enables these issues of power to be directly confronted. Arendt produced texts that challenged notions of freedom and politics, and notably examined the lives of people, ideas and historical events in ways that are pertinent to the purposes and practices of education.

This significant volume examines the main texts in the Arendt library and explains each of the key ideas and how they can enable critical thinking about knowledge production and practice in educational leadership. The analysis draws upon a range of exemplars and empirical projects from the field of educational leadership, investigating utility issues regarding Arendt's ideas, and engaging with the debates concerning her insights and contribution.

Included in the book:

- using Arendt to think about ELMA
- the relationship between policy and practice, and organisation and leadership
- critiques of the *vita activa* and *vita contemplativa*
- thinking with and against Arendt.

Gunter uses the work of Arendt to challenge the purposes and practices of intellectual work, with a view to developing perspectives on the responsibility for research and ideas. The book will be of value to all those working and researching in the field of Educational Leadership, Management and Administration.

Helen M. Gunter is Professor of Education Policy at the University of Manchester, UK.

Critical Studies in Educational Leadership, Management and Administration Series
Series Editors: Pat Thomson, Helen M. Gunter and Jill Blackmore

This series draws on social and political theories from selected key thinkers and activists to develop critical thinking leadership tools. Each text uses the work of a particular theorist or theoretical approach, explains the theory, suggests what it might bring to the ELMA field, and then offers analysis and case studies to show how the tools might be used. Every book also offers a set of questions that might be used by individual leaders in their own practices, and in areas of further research by ELMA scholars.

In elaborating the particular approaches, each of the books also suggests a professional and political agenda which addresses aspects of the tensions and problems created by neoliberal and neoconservative policy agendas, and the on-going need for educational systems to do better for many more of their students than they do at present.

Titles in the series
Deconstructing Educational Leadership: Derrida and Lyotard
Richard Niesche

Educational Leadership and Hannah Arendt
Helen M. Gunter

Educational Leadership and Michel Foucault
Donald Gillies

Educational Leadership and Hannah Arendt

Helen M. Gunter

Routledge
Taylor & Francis Group

LONDON AND NEW YORK

First published 2014
by Routledge
2 Park Square, Milton Park, Abingdon, Oxon OX14 4RN

Simultaneously published in the USA and Canada
by Routledge
711 Third Avenue, New York, NY 10017

Routledge is an imprint of the Taylor & Francis Group, an informa business

British Library Cataloguing in Publication Data
A catalogue record for this book is available from the British Library

Library of Congress Cataloging in Publication Data
Gunter, Helen M., author.
    Educational leadership and Hannah Arendt / Helen M. Gunter.
        pages cm. – (Critical studies in educational leadership,
        management, and administration)
    1. Educational leadership – Political aspects.   2. Democracy and
    education.   3. Arendt, Hannah, 1906–1975.   I. Title.
    LB2806.G85 2013
    371.2–dc23

                                                                    2013001778

ISBN: 978–0–415–82002–8 (hbk)
ISBN: 978–0–203–40986–2 (ebk)

Typeset in Garamond
by RefineCatch Limited, Bungay, Suffolk

Printed and bound in Great Britain by
TJ International Ltd, Padstow, Cornwall

Contents

Series foreword

Imagine yourself walking into the foyer of the Department of Education, Victoria, Australia. In front of you is a wall on which a series of names are displayed ceiling to floor. You glance quickly and note the following: Edward de Bono, Richard Elmore, Michael Fullan, Andy Hargreaves, Maria Montessori, Linda Darling-Hammond, Daniel Goleman, Kenneth Leithwood. Now imagine yourself in England. You decide to go to the website of the state owned leadership research and training National College and you find a section called Key Thinkers. When the screen changes you find yourself looking at a list which contains many of the same names.

Today, both of these things have disappeared. The names on the wall in Victoria have been removed and the National College website has been revamped. But both were in place for some years. Seeing them made us wonder what was going on that the very same people were being lauded on both sides of the world. We noted that both lists were dominated by North American men. In the Australian case, no Australians were listed, and in the case of England, the English names were in a minority. Would this happen if we were exploring a leadership space or place in Los Angeles? In Edinburgh? In Cape Town? In Beijing? In Buenos Aires? In Toronto? It is interesting to think about where and where not we might see similar listings.

We are sure that we would not have found this 30 years ago. While there was an international circulation of educational ideas and texts, the development of a celebrity leadership culture promoted by international gurus with modernizing know-how is a new phenomenon. It is worth considering why this might be the case. We think immediately of four possible reasons.

1   Leadership now encompasses all aspects of 'continuous educational improvement'. All professionals (and increasingly children and young people as well) are identified as leaders, doing leading and exercising leadership. Headteachers, or principals, are deemed repositories of

leadership that they do or do not 'distribute' to others to enable 'delivery' to be 'maximized'. All educational professionals are spoken to or about as school leaders, often without reference to role titles, and so just about everyone is potentially included as consumers of leadership ideas and models.

2   There is now a much greater focus on leadership development. Education policymakers from the right and left suggest that if policies are to be implemented then they need leaders at the local level to make it happen. Many have also decided that they only need to provide directions for change and frameworks for what is to be done, then devolve the means to secure resources necessary to the local leader.

3   Systems now assume that they need to be seen to be using the 'world's best practice'. National governments are highly conscious of their place in international league tables and their national credibility rests on being able to show some kind of 'continued improvement'. They are extremely vulnerable to media portrayals of 'failing' schools and/or systems. They believe that there are international 'solutions' to local problems which may appear not dissimilar to problems in other jurisdictions.

4   There now seems to be a leadership industry made up of knowledge producers and popularizers located in private companies, universities and schools. This leadership industry has made significant interventions in all spheres of activity, including in education and in educational leadership. What is on offer from a select range of academics and consultants, the travelling leadership entrepreneurs, is a set of tailor-made as well as off the peg 'solutions' to individuals, organizations and governments. These solutions are sold as transnational, evidence-based and transferable.

The readiness of the leadership industry to provide policy and professional solutions creates a situation in which it seems, if one examines the kinds of training on offer to potential school leaders, that there is a one-best way to do leading and leadership, and to be a leader. The promotion of policy anxiety, leadership and entrepreneurial activity is not necessarily, we suggest, a virtuous circle. We call this conjunction the Transnational Leadership Package (TLP).

The emergence of the TLP

The TLP is not a homogeneous body of work or people. It is derived from different national and cultural settings. It draws on a range of intellectual histories and practice traditions in different national contexts within the field of educational leadership, management and administration (ELMA). There are distinct, but interrelated, intellectual lineages within the field of ELMA which can be backtracked from contemporary concerns to particular historical contexts and theoretical origins. We call these lineages, paradigms. ELMA paradigms cannot be easily disconnected from each other, either theoretically or chronologically, as different approaches were often developed differently in different places and at different times, in response to the failure, or lack of explanatory power, of earlier paradigms. The ELMA paradigms, each with their own internal logics, can be roughly depicted as:

1   The US adoption of the Ford manufacturing Taylorist principles of **scientific management** (standardization specialization, synchronization, concentration, maximization and centralization) as the 'factory model' to emulate in schooling during the 1920s. Its later renditions are the school effectiveness and school improvement movements (SESI), and this is now interlocked with education policy through the imposition, across the entire public sector, of private sector market principles in the form of New Public Management (NPM). The core principles underpinning the resulting managerialization and marketization of schooling are competition and compliance, efficiency and effectiveness. Numbers as school rankings and comparisons are central to this push.

2   The post-war **human relations** movement, again largely US driven. This movement recognized how supportive social relations and participative decision-making informed productivity. This human relations paradigm is re-emerging in the twenty-first century in the therapeutic turn where emotional intelligence, managing interpersonal relations and intercultural communication are now seen as core leadership skills rather than a display of weakness. This paradigm informs the move away from the provision of public services through institutions towards brokerage, contracts and partnerships. Notably it is visible in the contemporary organisational and pedagogic discourse about personalised provision.

3   The US **theory movement** of the 1960s sought to establish ELMA as a value-free science. This paradigm has been ever present in ELMA, but has gained new clout through the contemporary focus on large-scale quantitative studies, evidence-based/informed practice and data-driven decision-making. Prime examples of this contemporary trend are the involvement of TLP in the US No Child Left Behind policy, and Every Child Matters in England.

4   The **experiential or pragmatic perspective** of the UK tradition which derived from a strong practitioner orientation and apprenticeship model of leadership. This has recently re-emerged in the 'what works' discourse in England when leadership accreditation and training provisions were taken up by governments, and as teacher education is pushed back into schools.

5   The **socially critical, neo-Marxist and feminist perspectives**, emerging predominantly from the geographical margins of Australia, New Zealand and Canada during the 1980s and 1990s. These are now being reinvigorated with the revival of social justice as a leadership issue in the 2010s, given the marked growth of educational inequality in both developed and developing nation states. This book series is located within this tradition.

There is now a convergence of the ELMA paradigms. This has occurred at the same time as neoliberal policies have spread from the Anglophone nation states to Asia, the Middle East, Mexico, South Africa and South America. Key aspects of the neoliberalist agenda are virtually enforced by international bodies such as the IMF, World Bank and OECD, and results of international standardised testing such as PISA are now a crucial reference point for policymakers in most countries in the world. This policy spread has been made possible in part through the advocacy work of knowledge and know-how entrepreneurs whose activity informs and is sometimes commissioned by these international agencies. The result is that there is now a coming together of the ELMA paradigms through preferred models such as transformational leadership, which is simultaneously about delivery, an emotional commitment to the delivery, and a predictive evidenced-based process to delivering the delivery! Tactical and pragmatic mediations may occur in some countries, such as England, but in the main the ELMA paradigms inform and communicate vision and mission for localized implementation.

ELMA can now be understood as a transnational field of educational research, with a recognizable lexicon, key players and logics of practice. This is the case regardless of whether we are looking at the TLP, other ELMA scholars somewhat separate from it, or socially critical scholars. Across ELMA generally there is a trend towards both standardization and normalization as to what constitutes good leadership through the development of leadership training programmes and professional standards nationally – a shift away from post-occupancy professional development to leadership preparation, in some instances requiring certification. Scholars from the fifth paradigm are also positioned by these developments and engage in the kinds of critical, deconstructive and reconstructive work that is the purpose of this book series. Indeed we have briefed our authors to engage in this process so that the problematization of the field of ELMA and its relationship with the TLP are central to the engagement with theory and theorizing.

The convergence of ELMA paradigms has also been actively produced by particular scholars and professionals through a process of selective eclecticism and appropriation of a set of concepts in response to the multiple and complex challenges of school leadership and to opportunities offered by anxious governments. This production, products and producers are what we refer to as the TLP.

The TLP is not the same as ELMA. It brings together concepts and practices that were formerly confined to particular localities and institutions into a particular 'saleable' form. The result is an assemblage of ideas and activities that focus primarily on the needs of educational systems and national governments. These do not necessarily meet the needs of individual schools, their students or their communities. The package is in fact constantly repackaged, and contains a few genuinely new ideas but plenty of normative rhetoric about the urgency to buy and use.

The TLP consists of three mutually supporting strands:

1   A set of policy prescriptions based on the experiences of consultants working in contractual (and often informal) partnerships with governments and agencies in particular jurisdictions, mostly North America and England, but also now including PISA success story, Finland. There are ready-made sound bites in this strand combined with the authority of 'best practice'.

2   A series of meta-analyses and effectiveness studies, whose impressive statistical manipulations mostly boil down to saying that if you want to improve students' learning then you have to focus on how teachers and classroom practice can 'deliver' higher outcome standards – and not on networks, teams or devolution of funding since these alone won't produce the desired test result improvements.

3   A cultural professional deficit where the identification of problems, agenda setting and strategizing is often perceived as rightly located outside of the school, and where notions of professional agency are reduced to tactical localized delivery. However some TLP manifestations have taken up the Finland exemplar to argue that a well-qualified and intellectually active teaching force is vital, and that too much emphasis on testing and league tabling is counter-productive. However, the role of leaders remains the same in both versions, as does the primary goal of meeting system needs.

The TLP provides a kind of (largely) Anglocentric policy IKEA flat-pack of policy 'levers' that will produce the actions and effects that count in national elections and international testing. While modern but cheap, it is worth 'buying into' largely because to be seen as different is risky.

However, there is considerable debate about whether these objectives meet the needs of schools, communities, teachers and students in countries as diverse as Denmark, New Zealand, South Africa, Canada, Wales and Singapore. At a time when populations in many countries are also becoming more diverse and less egalitarian, it is not clear that the TLP is up to the challenge.

We are not arguing here that the international circulation of ideas and people is to be discouraged. Obviously, finding out what others are doing can be very helpful as a means of generating new perspectives. The debate and discussion that occur when people with different positions come together are a Good Thing. However, we think it is ironic that at the same time as national governments and transnational agencies are concerned to maintain diversity of plants, animals and habitats, precisely the opposite is occurring with education policy ideas and practices. 'Good' leadership features prominently among one-best global prescriptions and representations. Many ELMA scholars not in the TLP, including those from critical paradigms, suggest that there is no one best way of leading or changing a school and that the models of transnational 'success' need to promote diverse approaches that are tailored to local needs histories and circumstances.

We take the view that what is needed in education is more than PISA envy and 'what works'. Prescribing a set of steps that governments and leaders can take, regardless of whereever and whoever they are, eliminates one of the most significant educational resources we have – our capacity to understand, analyse and imagine within our local contexts. It is a fine irony that these intellectual practices are precisely the ones that education systems are designed to inculcate in the next generation.

In these times, those who are engaged in *educational* leadership need, more than ever, to think about their work – its purposes and processes as well as its effects and outcomes. Our emphasis is on the *educational* where the knowledge, skills and processes that constitute professional practice are located in teaching and learning; these provide the basis for leading and managing. This series of books aims to support this kind of reflective *educational* work. Each volume will focus on the conceptual tools and methodologies of particular social science theory and theorists. We draw on scholarship from sociology, anthropology, philosophy, politics and cultural studies in order to interrogate, interrupt and offer alternative ideas to the contemporary versions of TLP and the broader field of ELMA.

The series provides theoretical and methodological options for those who are engaged in the formal study of educational leadership, management and administration. It provides alternative resources for naming, framing and acting for those who are engaged in the practice of educational leadership, management or administration, or who are providing training and policy for practising educational leaders.

The books series and critical thinking tools

This series of books might at first glance seem to be very removed from the kinds of pressures that we have described. However, our motivation for generating the series is highly practical. As series editors, we come to and, we hope, have informed the field of ELMA from different intellectual and occupational histories.

Together we take the view that now, more than ever, leading any educational institution requires intellectual work. Educational professionals must, in our view, be able not simply to follow policy prescriptions. In order to do the work of leading and leadership, educational professionals need to be able to: critically analyse policy directions; assess and evaluate their own institution and its local national and international contexts; not only understand how and why particular educational issues come to be centre stage while others are sidelined but also communicate this to others; call on a rich set of ideas in order to develop directions for the institution in particular and for education more generally. This requires, among other things, a set of critical thinking tools. These are not all that are required, but they are an essential component of professional practice.

This series draws on social and political theories from selected key thinkers and activists to develop some critical thinking leadership tools. Each text uses the work of a particular theorist or theoretical approach, explains the theory, suggests what it might bring to the ELMA field, and then offers analysis and case studies to show how the tools might be used. Each book also offers a set of questions that might be used by individual leaders in their own practices and some possible areas for further research by ELMA scholars.

In elaborating the particular approaches, each of the books also suggests a professional and political agenda which addresses aspects of the tensions and problems created by neoliberal and neoconservative policy agendas and by the ongoing need for educational systems to do better for many more of their students than they do at present.

Pat Thomson, Helen Gunter and Jill Blackmore
Series Editors

Acknowledgements

I would like to thank the ESRC for funding the two projects that are used to support the intellectual and empirical work reported in this particular book: Knowledge Production in Educational Leadership (KPEL) project (RES-000-23-1192) and Distributed Leadership and the Social Practices of School Organisation in England (SPSO) project (RES-000-22-3610). I would also like to thank David Hall who led the SPSO project, and for his co-authorship of Chapter 5. Thank you also to Geoff Bright and Steve Rogers for their insightful feedback. While I am indebted to a range of people who have helped me to think and write productively, I take full responsibility for the text.

This book is dedicated to the memory of Jill Bristow. The children, parents and staff of Alsager School have lost not only a superb teacher but someone who invested a life's work in the idea and practice of public education and the comprehensive school.

1 Introducing Hannah Arendt

Introduction

Hannah Arendt died of a heart attack on 4 December 1975. She was 69 years of age. She left an impressive intellectual legacy that continues to act as a provocation to think about current human predicaments in fresh and challenging ways. For example, her writings continue to speak to understandings of political protest (e.g. the Hungarian uprisings of 1956, Eastern Europe in 1989 and the Arab Spring from 2011), and so for Canovan (1998: vii) 'Hannah Arendt is pre-eminently the theorist of beginnings. All her books are tales of the unexpected (whether concerned with the novel horrors of totalitarianism or the new dawn of revolution), and reflections on the human capacity to start something new pervade her thinking'. However, her political and historical analysis remains controversial: Miller (1995: unpaged) reports that in response to *Eichmann in Jerusalem* (Arendt 1963), 'Walter Laqueur suggested that it was not so much what she had said, but how she said it: "the Holocaust is a subject that has to be confronted in a spirit of humility; whatever Mrs Arendt's many virtues, humility was not one of them".'

For Fraser (2004) 'Hannah Arendt was the greatest theorist of mid-20th-century catastrophe,' and she locates her as follows (2004: 253):

> Writing in the aftermath of the Nazi holocaust, she taught us to conceptualize what was at stake in this darkest of historical moments. Seen through her eyes, the extermination camps represented the most radical negation of the quintessentially human capacity for spontaneity and the distinctively human condition of plurality. Thus, for Arendt they had a revelatory quality. By taking to the limit the project of rendering superfluous the human being as such, the Nazi regime crystallized in the sharpest and most extreme way humanity-threatening currents that characterized the epoch more broadly.

Having experienced totalitarianism, loss of freedom and statelessness as a refugee, Arendt's political and historical analysis enables understandings of the relationship between thinking and practice. So a biographical 'sketch' as an opening to this book is less about a contextual vignette, or even a decorative start, and is more about how Arendt's contribution to intellectual work is integral to a lived life. This therefore prompts myself as author and you as reader to consider how location within knowledge production is itself a political and historical issue, and how reading and engaging with Arendt's life and work continues to resonate with ourselves nearly a century after her birth.

The aim of this book is to examine the politics of knowledge production through reading education policy and practice regarding ELMA using Arendt's methods and ideas. In doing this I agree with Canovan (1995: 281) that 'the most fruitful way of reading her political thought is, I believe, to treat her analysis of modernity as a context for the interesting things she has to say about the fact that politics goes on among plural persons with space between them'. The key questions to be addressed for the field of ELMA are to do with giving recognition to a plurality within field research, theory and professional practice: the type of knowledge that travels from one context to another, how particular ideas are accepted and used, the debates that take place, the existence and quality of theorising and the funding of research. In this opening chapter I intend to set the scene by introducing Hannah Arendt as a person, thinker and activist, and exploring how her approach to politics and history is useful for how the current challenges for the social sciences in general and public education in particular are debated.

Hannah Arendt

Hannah Arendt was born in Hanover in 1906 into a well-educated left-wing home. She grew up strongly independent, relished intellectual work and she was a student of both Heidegger and Jaspers. After she married Günther Stern in 1929 she moved to Berlin, and following the Reichstag Fire she became increasingly involved in the resistance. After being arrested, interrogated and released, she left Germany for Prague, then Geneva and finally Paris, where she met her second husband, Heinrich Blücher. They were interned as enemy aliens in France, and in 1941 they fled to the USA, where Arendt became a citizen in 1951. Consequently, there is a need to recognise, as Miller (1995: unpaged) does, that 'Arendt's life straddled two continents, bringing into contact two quite different intellectual cultures (and producing endless opportunities for misunderstanding)'. Scholars have provided accounts of Arendt's life and work (see Baehr 2003, Bowring 2011, Young-Bruehl 1982, Watson 1992), so here I will draw out some important themes and messages that will both enable the reading of this book, and let us think about how Arendt's life and work speaks to researching and conceptualising educational issues.

Education did not capture Arendt's prime attention in regard to major writing projects but she did engage in a number of ways, not least as a school student:

> Headstrong and independent, she displayed a precocious aptitude for the life of the mind. And while she might risk confrontation with a teacher who offended her with an inconsiderate remark – she was briefly expelled for leading a boycott of the teacher's classes – from German *Bildung* (cultivation) there was to be no rebellion.
>
> (Baehr 2003: viii)

During her expulsion she studied at the University of Berlin, taking classes in Greek, Latin and theology, and following the completion of school she studied at the universities of Marburg and Heidelberg (Bowring 2011). University provided her with an intellectual community and was a time when she was further politicised, not least through how she used her apartment in Berlin to hide political refugees. Just as she had faced the consequences of activism in school by being excluded, she experienced this as an adult, where she found herself variously detained and then released by the police in Berlin, transported to an internment camp in France, and then escaped to New York. This interplay between academic and political life is evident through her work as a journalist, author, editor, researcher and university teacher in Chicago and New York. Baehr (2003: vii) illuminates this by arguing that while she was a private person, she did confront issues in ways that generated controversy:

> A Jew who in the 1930s and forties campaigned tirelessly on behalf of Zionism . . . Arendt opposed the formation of a unitary Israeli state. And how, given commonplace modes of thought, are we to cope with a theorist who documented the twentieth century's fundamental rupture with tradition, while championing the notions of truth, facts, and common sense? Or with an author of one of the masterpieces of political 'science' – *The Origins of Totalitarianism* (1951) – who expressed the strongest reservations about social science in general?

This is also evident in her writing on education, where she confronts bigger issues of the politics and history of the republic: so she articulated a *Crisis in Education* (Arendt 2006a) through a concern with the decline in authority; and in 1957 she wrote *Reflections on Little Rock* (Arendt 2003) in which she opposed the ruling by the Supreme Court on school desegregation because of the implications for the positioning of children in the political process.

So Arendt's work is political and historical (Calhoun and McGowan 1997), with claims that she is a philosopher (Watson 1992), but she was an espoused political scientist (Kohn 1994): 'she saw her work as directed to political decision making in the present: here, "between past and future," all of us should be deciding how to act and how to live' (Barta 2007: 88), and interestingly she described herself as 'something between a historian and a publicist' (quoted in Benhabib 2000: ix). Young-Bruehl (1982) entitles her biography *For Love of the World* as a means of illuminating Arendt's 'concerns for the world' (1982: x), and Canovan (1995: 276) emphasises the message that people should be politically responsible in their lives: it is 'our duty to be citizens, looking after the world and taking responsibility for what is done in our name'; she goes on to argue that if Arendt:

> was a harsh critic of political irresponsibility under the conditions of pre-war Germany, it is not surprising that she had even less patience with American citizens who enjoyed the blessing of a free constitution, but who were too immersed in their private consumption to notice what use was being made of their power.
>
> (Canovan 1995: 276)

In claiming that freedom is located in the spaces between people where political issues can be worked through, and in modelling such freedom through the debates she generated and participated in, then Arendt resisted categorisation. She has been labelled as both liberal and conservative. It seems that, as Baehr (2003: vii) identifies, Arendt 'was a deeply paradoxical figure', not least that 'she was among the greatest women political thinkers of the twentieth century, yet one strikingly at odds with academic feminism' (pvii). Her work has stimulated productive thinking and debate in education (Gordon 2001a) and genocide studies (Stone 2011), but at the same time silences (King 2011) and contradictions (Butler and Spivak 2010) have been identified in such a way that Baum *et al.* (2011: 7) note that Arendt was 'viewed as a figure very much of her own time'. However, the renaissance in her work is explained by scholars because of her contribution to a range of debates about the condition of political life (Benhabib 2000), and Baum *et al.* (2011: 8) conclude that: 'there are ways in which Arendt's thought has been rehabilitated by the left in the service of a critique of the contemporary neoliberal state and its totalitarian tendencies'. This book is located in this critical tradition, as I intend to relate the growth and trends in knowledge production within ELMA to wider issues of politics and governance.

Reading and thinking with Hannah Arendt

Giving due respect to the focus on politics and the controversies that her work generated, and finding a way through her writings in order to appropriately engage with the ideas and context, is a key task of my role as an author. Following Canovan's (1995) example I will not attempt to systemise her thinking by constructing and imposing a rationale that Arendt did not herself create. Instead I will 'try to follow the windings and trace the interconnections of her thinking' (Canovan 1995: 12) as a means of engaging with her ideas and methods.

Arendt produced a body of work that is both conceptual and realistic, and can be variously and simultaneously descriptive, critical and experimental. She wrote major texts and published collections of essays, the bulk in her lifetime, but much was published posthumously, and this book will draw on a range of these works, as illustrated in Table 1.

Such a listing presents an impressive body of work but without engaged reading it is sterile, mainly because Arendt speaks to and about major issues pertinent to the social sciences. A challenge is where to start. Some writers begin with *The Human Condition* (Arendt 1958) and 'this view argues that Hannah Arendt is a political philosopher of nostalgia, an anti-modernist lover of the Greek polis' (Benhabib 2000: xxxix). However, Benhabib (2000), Young-Bruehl (2006) and Canovan (1995) all argue that

Table 1.1 Hannah Arendt's key works used in this book

Title of text	Date first published	Date of edition used in this book
The Origins of Totalitarianism	1951	2009
Between the Past and Future	1954	2006a
Essays in Understanding 1930–1954	1954	1994
Men in Dark Times	1955	1993
The Human Condition	1958	1958
Eichmann in Jerusalem	1963	2005
On Revolution	1963	2006b
Crises of the Republic	1969	1972
On Violence	1969	1970
Life of the Mind	1971	1978
Responsibility and Judgement	2003	2003
The Promise of Politics	2005	2005

the starting point is *The Origins of Totalitarianism* (Arendt 2009), because 'responses to the most dramatic events of her time lie at the very centre of Arendt's thought' (Canovan 1995: 7).

So in illuminating her work I will follow this approach, and re-emphasise how she worked on action and the plurality of political life. For Arendt action is political and public. Politics is space and needs space, it is where the person describes the self, where discussion happens and where the possibilities of 'natality' (Arendt 1958) can be realised. People are helped in this process by institutions as a legitimising, durable and stabilising framework through which the initiative and accommodation of the plural person can happen. What is needed to hold the common together are places where people can be separate but at the same time connected, like sitting at a table. When those spaces are removed, and people are essential-ised into a type, then totalitarianism can be experienced. *The Origins of Totalitarianism* afforded Arendt the opportunity to analyse this, and while she recognised that such a regime could be defeated from external forces such as the use of military action to end the Third Reich, she struggled with the possibility that internal conditions could enable change. While she showed optimism about human capacity to do the unpredictable, it was change within the Soviet Union following the death of Stalin that led her to argue that regimes can be internally transformed. Of interest to issues discussed in this book is to develop understandings of ELMA in relation to the conditions that produce education policy, particularly about whether and how educational professionals do some-thing new as action.

A second example comes from her attendance at and subsequent reporting of the Eichmann trial in Jerusalem (Arendt 1963), where as a journalist she sought to understand the processes that had enabled total-itarian tendencies to become a reality. Notably she argued that his actions were not based on an ideology as such but on a 'deficit of thought' or what she labelled his 'banality'. Arendt gave attention to Eichmann's careerism, and how he justified his actions on the basis of following orders. Of interest to issues discussed in this book is to develop understandings of ELMA in relation to those who practise it, and how engagement with reforms that do damage to education and children could be characterised as following orders.

In a third example, *The Human Condition* (Arendt 1958), she distin-guishes between and examines labour, work and action. Labour is neces-sary to produce what a human needs to survive; work produces goods that are more durable and hence stabilise the social. Humans produce, and their products can outlast the processes that produced them and the objective for which they were produced. Humans therefore live amongst and with each other, and action with others requires the presentation and understanding of who the person is. Of interest to issues discussed in this book is to develop understandings of ELMA as labour, work and action, and I intend to examine Arendt's (1958) contention that labour has come to dominate.

These brief encounters with just three texts show that Arendt engaged with the individual and the polity. While her writings specifically focus on Nazism, Stalinism, the Holocaust and nuclear weapons, she thought about the bigger issues of the human condition through examining the central issues of her time, and she kept on thinking about and refining her use of language and perspectives on events. It seems that she liked to watch the news and often shouted at the TV, and this is a helpful motif for understanding her approach:

> it is tempting to say that she brought philosophy to bear on events; but the truth appears to have been more nearly the opposite. It was events that set her mind in motion, and philosophy that had to adjust . . . her thinking seems to 'crystallize' (the word is hers) around events, like a coral reef branching outward, one thought leading to another. The result is an independent body of coherent but never systematically ordered reflection that, while seeming to grow from within over her lifetime, according to laws and principles peculiar to itself, at the same time manages to continually illuminate contemporary affairs.
>
> (Schell 2006: xii)

Methodologically Arendt was interested in how ideas and writing could generate understandings that could be debated in the polity; she wrote about the plurality of people and ideas, and operated on the basis that this was worth taking action for:

> What is important for me is to understand. For me, writing is a matter of seeking this understanding, part of the process of understanding . . . what is important for me is the thought process itself. As long as I have succeeded in thinking something through, I am personally quite satisfied. If I then succeed in expressing my thought processes adequately in writing, that satisfies me also.
>
> (Arendt 1994: 3)

Three main methods of generating understanding have been identified: first, she examined the meaning of words and the conditions to which they were applied, and so in *The Human Condition* she makes a distinction between labour, work and action: 'Arendt wanted thoughts and words adequate to the new world and able to dissolve clichés, reject thoughtlessly received ideas, break down hackneyed analyses, expose lies and bureaucratic doubletalk, help people withdraw from their addiction to propagandistic images' (Young-Bruehl 2006: 11). Second, following Walter Benjamin, she used what Benhabib (2000: x) calls a 'fragmentary historiography', where 'one treats the past by acting either as a collector or as a pearl diver, digging down for those treasures that lie now disjointed and disconnected' (Benhabib 2000: 173). Third, Arendt rejects causality and the inevitability of events, and instead presents a 'crystallization' of historical factors as a means of explaining totalitarianism; King (2007: 253) argues this was 'shrewdly chosen' because:

> the process of crystallization can hardly be perceived as taking place *over* time, as opposed to happening in the shortest historical duration, *within* a moment of time. Seen in this light, 'crystallization' happens in and because of the 'interruption' of the historical continuum.

So in *The Origins of Totalitarianism* she not only distinguishes between totalitarianism and tyranny, but examines the relationship between the situation in Nazi Germany and Stalinist Soviet Union through problematising anti-semitism, colonialism and imperialism (Stone 2011). Consequently, Arendt is regarded as 'a practical-minded person who used distinction making to break things down into their component parts and show how they worked' (Young-Breuhl 2006: 11). This was not only a personal preference regarding how she wanted to think and write, but also recognition that totalitarian regimes had challenged the human condition in such a way that the traditional categories and ways of thinking just did not do the job any more. In doing this she not only presented scholarly analysis but also told stories: 'but she, I think, thought that the well-chosen anecdote was worth a thousand statistics or citations or evidences' (Young-Bruehl and Kohn 2001: 228).

While researchers might locate totalitarianism as events in the past, Arendt's approach was to recognise that the conditions from which it developed remain contemporary, and so there is a need to understand the precarious situation in which the human condition is located (Kohn 1994). At the same time there is a need to challenge flawed comparisons between the past and present, where 9/11 is not the same as Pearl Harbor. However, in response to 9/11 YoungBruehl (2006) shows how *The Origins of Totalitarianism* can be used to interrogate the state of the republic through challenging the response by the Bush administration with a 'war on terror' and 'homeland security'. Similarly Mayer (2009) identifies that it would be wrong to suggest 'any moral equivalence between the Nazis and the Bush Administration' but she identifies how documents reveal the detailed CIA discussions of torture, and how currently the Obama administration is finding it hard to pin down responsibility due to what Arendt (1970) called 'rule by Nobody': 'those on the top can claim to have clean hands, while those on the bottom can claim they were following ostensibly legal orders. What's left, Arendt suggests, is an all-powerful government that is beyond accountability' (Mayer 2009: unpaged). Thinking with Arendt in this way is not the unreflexive transfer of analysis from one moment in time to another, or the co-option of labels, it is about identifying what is new about a situation that enables understanding. In this book I do not intend to compare Stalinist Russia with contemporary professional practices in schools in England, but I do intend to use Arendt's analysis of catastrophe to reveal the catastrophe within and for those schools.

Arendt is not a problem solver: 'she emphatically denied that her role as a political thinker was to propose a blueprint for the future or to tell anyone what to do' (Canovan 1998: viii); rather, she is a problem poser. So 'political analysis for her was less a matter of culling lessons from the past than of being able to identify what was new, which calls for a new, creative response' (YoungBruehl 2006: 61). So a rule book with the answers to every question is not possible. In 1966 in the midst of the Vietnam war, Arendt stated:

> Particular questions must receive particular answers; and if the series of crises in which we have lived since the beginning of the century can teach us anything at all, it is, I think, the simple fact that there are no general standards to determine our judgements unfailingly, no general rules under which to subsume the particular cases with any degree of certainty.
>
> (Quoted in Kohn 2003: vii)

She addresses situations, looks at them from different positions, makes judgements and can show anger at what she witnesses:

> This does not mean she wanted to believe it possible to hand over her own thoughts to anyone else. That would have been sheer nonsense to Arendt, for whom thinking – understanding, endowing an event with meaning – was an engagement with oneself, solitary and private.
>
> (Kohn 1994: x–xi)

Her rage, with sometimes an abrasive or tactless approach, has been recognised as understandable. Swift (2011: 80–81) notes that in writing about the concentration camps it was not possible for Arendt to construct a form of fabricated objectivity as this would condone what had happened:

> The angry style of *The Origins of Totalitarianism* resists such a move by insisting on the particularity of totalitarianism. The book's insistence and anger account for the peculiarly divergent types of emotional tone that its earliest readers found in it . . . being 'praised as passionate and criticized as sentimental'.

Furthermore, Butler (Butler and Spivak 2010) talks about trying to find Arendt in a text through the use of 'I' when she seems to use 'we', and she argues that this 'displacement' is not unexpected because she is writing about this 'as an exile, in the wake of her own displacement' (ibid.: 28).

It seems that saying things that need to be said generates honest analysis, where thinking and judgement enables the reality of a situation to be uncovered. Arendt was criticised for a lack of 'love for the Jewish people' (Swift 2011: 81), and this raises questions about how a researcher positions the self. For Arendt, such 'love' is not possible or necessary regarding a group of people or a nation:

> the rules of tact and social decorum are always in principle sacrificable, in Arendt's argument, to contact with reality, and the hope for a politics which might grow out of it. To this extent, anger . . . could be understood as a healthy symptom of the political self's desire to make contact with reality, to push through sentimental, guilty and narcissistic responses to suffering in order to uncover what the politically real might be. Such anger, both in the style of political writing and in political action, might risk appearing heartless and tactless, but then a loving, heartfelt response to the world is something of a contradiction in Arendt's terms anyway.
>
> (Swift 2011: 92)

In doing this, she incentivises the researcher 'to think for oneself' (Kohn 2003: xi), she demonstrates the responsibility that she expected political scientists to take. Indeed, she was horrified by how intellectuals went along with Nazism as a form of *Gleichschaltung* or co-operated with the new political world as a means of protecting a job or position: 'I left Germany dominated by the idea – of course somewhat exaggerated: Never again! I shall never again get involved in any kind of intellectual business . . . I thought that it had to do with this profession, with being an intellectual' (Arendt 1994: 11). So through her work she models the plurality within political life that she argues in favour of.

In giving recognition to the value of her work, Baehr (2003: vii) argues that:

> such fearless originality indicates that Hannah Arendt was 'one of those writers who is well worth stealing'. But it is a relatively simple thing to appropriate a person's ideas, quite another to cultivate the 'willed independence of judgment' and 'conscious distance from all fanaticisms' that animated them.

Based on intellectual work located in a combination of experience, beliefs and reading, Arendt constructs arguments that speak to and about the modern world. She stimulates thinking through scholarly analysis:

> Arendt possesses the surprisingly rare, and rather unsettling, ability to make you, or rather to make you want to, think. This sounds like an anodyne observation. After all, aren't we all, academics, intellectuals and students, in the full-time business of thinking? Universities are full of very clever people, but Arendt makes clear – first in the style of her writing and reasoning, and second in the explicit analysis of humans' mental faculties that she developed in her later work – that cognition and thinking are not the same thing. What she seemed to learn most from her study of Adolf Eichmann is that intelligent people are able to do the most awful things, and that cleverness does not immunise us against thoughtlessness and the temptation to do wrong. Arendt's own determination to think through, clarify, and then judge the human component in the most inhuman of events and deeds is perhaps the most challenging and controversial of her intellectual gifts.
>
> (Bowring 2011: 4)

Notably, Arendt's writing is about taking action and taking responsibility for those actions through how she thinks out loud (Canovan 1998), engages in 'mental gymnastics' (Kohn 2006: xvii) and exercises judgement (Kirsch 2009) about the meaning of events and ideas, and she does this through major monograph projects, as well as through book reviews and replies to reviews of her work.

Nevertheless, her work faces opposition, particularly since 'Hannah Arendt remains a fiercely independent mind whose work defies classification in terms of established schools of political thought' (Benhabib 2000: xxxvi). There are those who are deeply offended by her judgements, those who just don't recognise the value of making distinctions, and 'many social scientists, of course, look down their noses at Arendt's method as anecdotal' (Young-Bruehl and Kohn 2001: 228). Reading Arendt can be a challenge:

Arendt's books invite misunderstanding, for they are often condensed and allusive. Their form is symphonic rather than sequential, interweaving and developing themes rather than presenting an argument. She often tries to say more (and particularly to make more conceptual distinctions) than can be comfortably digested, and since she does not warn her readers before using ordinary terms in special senses, it is very easy to miss the significance of what she is saying, particularly when (as is often the case) she is saying something unexpected.

(Canovan 1995: 3)

In the introduction to *The Human Condition*, Canovan (1998: viii) states: 'here is a long, complex piece of writing that conforms to no established pattern, crammed with unexpected insights but lacking a clearly apparent argumentative structure'. In addition to this Benhabib (2000) raises questions about the use of language and how this can lead to misreading: first, the use of 'banal' needs attention in regard to Eichmann: 'Arendt did not mean that Eichmann's cooperation in the extermination of the Jews, and of other peoples, by the Nazis was banal. She referred rather to a specific quality of mind and character of the doer himself' (ibid.: 176). Second, the use of 'thoughtlessness' in regard to Eichmann troubled Mary McCarthy who edited her work and who 'complains, not for the first time, about Arendt's tendency to force the English language to mean what it does not mean' (ibid.: 177).

So there is a need to examine: why was she read, why is she still read and why is her work used? Positioning by myself as author requires that such questions are interrelated with the bigger picture of knowledge production and the power processes that mean, for example, that Shakespeare is on the school curriculum in England but other writers either never got there or have long since disappeared. A text is not worthy in its own right, it matters because of the political practices of human beings to purchase it, to read it, to think while using it and to act as a result of it. An idea, a book, a lecture is given status and distinction through the acclaim of others, who bestow recognition as being important, and in need of time and attention. What is interesting is that Arendt has not led to an 'ism' such as Marxism, has not led to the decoration of texts with soundbites such as 'discourse' in the way that Foucault is often used (or misused). At the same time her work has not been waiting on a shelf to be discovered, as it has been read and engaged with.

Increased recognition can generate attention in ways that can lead to fashionable quoting and referencing rather than substantial engagement:

If Arendt matters today, it is because of her writings on imperialism, Zionism and careerism. Composed during the 1940s and early 1960s, they not only challenge facile and fashionable applications of the total-itarianism thesis; they also eerily describe the dangers that the world now faces. By refusing to reckon with these writings, the journalists, intellectuals and academics who make up the Arendt industry betray her on two counts: they ignore an entire area of her work and fail to engage with the unsettling realities of their own time.

(Robin 2007: unpaged)

The irony is that as Robin (2007: unpaged) has argued 'academic careers are built on interpretations of her work', but as he has shown in her account of the Eichmann trial, such 'careerism . . . is seldom conducive to thinking'. Her account of the trial (Arendt 1963) was and remains provocative, and so she is known for this book and known about in regard to the way this book is written and spoken about. So the phrase 'banality of evil' is often evoked to make news headlines, for example Young-Bruehl (2006) shows how it has been used to decorate major stories, such as the comparison of Eichmann with Saddam Hussein in the US media, without due respect to the intellectual origins of what Arendt actually meant by 'banality' and 'evil'. She goes on to say:

If the phrase 'the banality of evil' is removed from the soundbite circuit, unpacked, explored, used as a catalyst for thought, held up as a lens, well then, it becomes more interesting, more challenging – it signifies a great deal. And if it is directed at Hannah Arendt's oeuvre, it will take you right to the core of her thinking, right to her abiding preoc-cupations, to the small cluster of hugely significant thoughts that she thought and rethought for all of her adult life. And it is because of these ideas and the example of how she used them that Arendt matters for us, now, as thinking and acting people, as citizens.

(Young-Bruehl 2006: 5)

Arendt has faced the tendency to be known and known about even though she has only been met through the written word rather than in person, and the proclivity to read just one edition of a text, or select just aspects of that text, can lead to the essentialising of the oeuvre:

'She was hailed, justifiably, as both a liberal wanting change and a conservative desiring stability, and has been criticized for haboring an unrealistic yearning for the past or for being a utopian revolutionary' (Kohn 1994: x).

Arendt is not the first person to resist and be irritated by this (see Bourdieu 1990) but it does illuminate how a person takes responsibility:

> 'You know the left think I am a conservative,' Hannah Arendt once said, 'and the conservatives think I am left or I am a maverick or God knows what. And I must say that I couldn't care less. I don't think the real questions of this century get any kind of illumination by this kind of thing.'
>
> (Butler 2007: unpaged)

While she was alive Arendt was able to engage in debates through replying to critics, and so in facing critiques about her account of Jewish councils which cooperated with the Nazis, she states:

> To begin, I want to comment on the rather furious controversy touched off by my book, *Eichmann in Jerusalem*. I deliberately use the words 'touched off,' rather than the word 'caused,' for a large part of the controversy was devoted to a book that was never written.
>
> (Arendt 2003: 17)

The danger is that once a person is dead their work can be conserved as a 'canon' with followers who pronounce on the veracity of interpretations, with potential schisms and sects. An analysis of the politics of knowledge production is therefore vital to understanding this task, as the author can no longer take responsibility for her work, and so it falls to others to do this.

The contribution of this book

The focus on knowledge production through using Arendt's political and historical thinking is a contribution I would like to make to the social sciences in general as well as the ELMA field specifically. My argument is that Arendt's approach can provoke ideas, meanings and understandings for the social sciences by examining the interrelationship between plural persons generating ideas and taking action, and can illuminate the dangers of substituting action with activity. Indeed, the challenge for ELMA is that there is too much activity based on limited and often non-educational ideas and/or common sense beliefs, and not enough action located in scholarly debates and research.

I would like to begin with a bigger picture analysis by presenting three news items in the UK media:

Story 1

The mother of a two-year-old girl who wandered off from a nursery yesterday relived the moment she found her drowning in a garden pond. Victoria Rae, 36, fought back tears as she told an inquest she jumped into the algae-covered water to recover what she thought was daughter Abigail's shoe. The mother – who had earlier been told by nursery staff searching for the toddler that they were looking for a dog – said: 'I reached forward to grab Abby's shoe which was towards the centre of the pond.' 'As I grabbed for the shoe, I missed the shoe and put my hand under the water and was shocked to touch what felt like a leg. I put my hands around the leg, which was around the calf area, and pulled the leg upwards. As I did this, I saw that it was Abby I was pulling out. The rest is a bit of a blur.' Mrs Rae later wept as a brick-layer, who drove past Abby in his van as she walked through her village, explained he did not stop to help in case people thought he was trying to abduct her. Clive Peachey said: 'She wasn't walking in a straight line. She was tottering. I kept thinking, "Should I go back?" One reason I did not go back is because I thought someone would see me and think I was trying to abduct her. I was convinced her parents were driving around and had found her.'

(Chaytor 2006: unpaged)

Story 2

The turning of the memorial to merchant seamen drowned in the two world wars into a playground for revelling bankers this Christmas is hard to better as an example of the way we live now. Or as an argument against the way we live now. By allowing partying amid the monuments to the dead, the authorities are asserting three propositions that have become so accepted that we have forgotten to be shocked by them: that there's nothing that money cannot or should not be able to buy; that government can ignore any scruple in its search for revenue; and that no one can gainsay the determination of plutocrats to celebrate their self-enrichment as the highest form of human achievement . . . It applied for permission to cover the lawn of Trinity Square Gardens with a vast marquee. The roof will be transparent so carousers can gaze up to trees . . . the managing director, told me that no celebration was too extravagant for his company to contemplate. He could host feasts for 300, 400, 500 or more if required. How much per diner? I asked. It depends. If the customer wants the best food, the finest wines, the most expensive cocktails, he could supply them if the price was right. His tone became a tad defensive as I questioned him and I detected a note of puzzlement. The partygoers would not be dancing on top of the monuments but in the garden around them. He was proposing to free an illiquid asset and monetise what until now had been nothing but a worthless, if revered, patch of grass. Isn't that what anyone in his position would want to do and should want to do? . . . I cannot find a better way of explaining the fault of the bankers, the party organisers and bureaucrats than to say they lack proper modesty. Puffed up by a culture that celebrates self-enrichment they have no real sense of their significance. Like Charlie Gilmour when he swung on the Union flag at the Cenotaph, they do not understand that just because they are rich it does not mean that their lives are more worthwhile than the men and women who died without enjoying their advantages; that although it is a cliche to say that they died so the bankers, the Gilmours and the rest of us might be free, the cliche remains true for all the corniness it carries. But then I suppose 'those who have no grave but the sea' offer no opportunity for gain. You cannot turn them from an illiquid to a liquid asset, slice, dice and monetise them. The dead cannot generate an income, so all who want to make a profit can safely forget that they ever existed.

(Cohen 2011: unpaged)

Story 3

I would like to thank many people. My doctors, nurses and hospital staff who are doing all they can for me; the British Police who are pursuing my case with vigour and professionalism and are watching over me and my family. I would like to thank the British Government for taking me under their care. I am honoured to be a British citizen. I would like to thank the British public for their messages of support and for the interest they have shown in my plight. I thank my wife, Marina, who has stood by me. My love for her and our son knows no bounds. But as I lie here I can distinctly hear the beating of wings of the angel of death. I may be able to give him the slip but I have to say my legs do not run as fast as I would like. I think, therefore, that this may be the time to say one or two things to the person responsible for my present condition. You may succeed in silencing me but that silence comes at a price. You have shown yourself to be as barbaric and ruthless as your most hostile critics have claimed. You have shown yourself to have no respect for life, liberty or any civilised value. You have shown yourself to be unworthy of your office, to be unworthy of the trust of civilised men and women. You may succeed in silencing

one man but the howl of protest from around the world will rever-
berate, Mr Putin, in your ears for the rest of your life. May God forgive
you for what you have done, not only to me but to beloved Russia and
its people.

(Alexander Litvinenko in *The Independent*, 2006: unpaged)

These three stories all indicate that democracy with a principled and practical requirement for redress of grievance in England is healthy: there is an
open system of justice, there is investigative journalism, and a citizen who
has been poisoned can speak out in support of the inquiry that is under
way to find his murderers. And yet, each story illuminates some deeply
rooted problems in democratic culture and practice: that fear pervades
society in such a way as to generate fabrications and prevent a caring relationship between strangers; that what matters in society is the commer-
cialization of the dead, as a means of generating income and personal
enjoyment; and, that the nation state cannot protect its citizens.

An important contribution by the social sciences is to relate ideas and
actions to a wider context about how all three stories are concerned with
the decline of the civic project regarding the construction and development
of a healthy political fabric, and the increasing dominance of neoliberalism
through reform projects that facilitate the 'financialization of everything'
(Harvey 2007), and of neoconservativism through the generation of fear
(Furedi 2006). Hannah Arendt's thinking can contribute to this analysis:
notably that Story 1 is about the banality of the ways in which individual
decisions might be defended; Story 2 is about a failure of politics and the
public realm, and Story 3 is about the conditions from which totalitarianism develops, and how this mode of politics through a denial of politics
crosses borders.

Reading such stories evokes a response: the emotion of how the person
other than the self has been treated, particularly the innocent and those
unable to speak back, combined with the indignation of how this
was allowed to happen, who is to blame and how it might be prevented.
Tut-tutting at the breakfast table, comments made on the train, and even
lambasting the TV are possible responses. The transient nature of this, and
even immunity through the emotional saturation of 24/7 news, can also be
imagined. While social scientists are deeply involved in such issues, their
place and the particular contribution may not be seen as obvious or particularly relevant, as their questions and concerns can be positioned as
removed from the realities of the lives revealed through such tragic events.
Notably Apple (2011) talks about his position as teacher regarding the
pedagogic issues following the 9/11 events, with particular emphasis on
the challenges of enabling spaces for both anger and criticality. Carrying

on as normal did not seem to be an option for him, but at the same time he identifies the vulnerabilities in interrupting the mood of the moment in ways that could be interpreted as arrogant.

Delanty (1997) has troubled social science with a call to relate more directly to real problems as distinct from problems that professional researchers think matter. Recently Chakrabortty (2012) has claimed that academic elites have failed to respond to the banking crisis and instead continue to talk and write in ways disconnected from the taxpayer who funds their work. Arendt's position creates helpful understandings of how to think this through, because contrary to Delanty's (1997) position, she demonstrated the importance of distance and removal as a means of speaking about issues that have a history and a future that could outlast an individual's mortality. Writing and speaking on issues with scholarship and evidence does not automatically set an agenda as *the* agenda in ways that excludes the public; instead it embraces the public. If the people within the three stories or the people who read about them do not take forward their ideas into a debate, that does not invalidate someone such as Arendt from doing so: what it does is to speak about the condition of the polity and how people understand political life. The concern, as this book will show, is for politics to be conflated with government, and for governments to speak on behalf of the governed by appropriating knowledge production and knowledge workers to secure their short-term political goals (see Gunter 2012a). Arendt's biography and intellectual contribution to the social sciences demonstrates how knowledge production can be and needs to be both simultaneously distant and involved.

More needs to be said about this, and replies to Chakrabortty (2012) have identified the need to give recognition to the valuable intellectual work that is taking place, particularly at a time when managerialism with the drive to demonstrate 'cause and effect' measured impact can be experienced as suffocatingly totalising (Jordan 2012, McCann 2012). Gamble (2012), echoing Arendt's arguments about action, argues that Chakrabortty 'misunderstands the relationship between ideas and action' and:

> if we are to shift direction . . . we need not just a fundamental re-imagining of our political economy but also the building of a new coalition of interests which can force change. Academics as public intellectuals have a role in helping build that coalition, but ideas by themselves are never enough. We need politics too.
>
> (Gamble 2012: unpaged)

Political science continues to forensically uncover the way power structures operate in such a political process (e.g. Moran 2007, Saint-Martin

2000), and my own study of ELMA shows that knowledge production regarding what knowledge is recognised as being of worth, which methods of knowing are deemed valid, and which knowers are regarded as trustworthy, is a highly complex, shifting and politically fraught arena (Gunter 2012a).

This relationship between ideas and action is directly relevant for ELMA, and I would like to use an example of how Arendt's work can be deployed as a means of illuminating an important challenge for the field. Levinson (2002) uses Arendt to examine bullying in schools; he argues that it is constructed through the onlooker who does not take action, and this can be further understood through Arendt's analysis that Nazi and Stalinist terror was not just through the systems and practices of government but 'as a consequence of a profound failure on the part of most people to see themselves as active shapers of a shared world' (Levinson 2002: 200). This is pertinent for the ELMA field because the staff and students in a school (where misconduct is differentially labelled as bullying for children and harrassment for adults) may assume that they are exercising agency by solving problems through organisational leadership (or management or administrative) processes. Activity through making interventions in practice by designing and building commitment to policies is important, but an organisational policy cannot of itself resolve entrenched social conflicts and dysfunctional conduct. So instrumental problem solving may enable people to be visibly seen to be doing something, but this can prevent the 'onlookers' as followers from engaging with more critical ideas and taking action. Consequently, the ideas in this book may interrupt such activity, because using Arendt enables particular purposes, rationales and narratives to be open to scrutiny, and to be challenged in ways that generate action located in the plurality of persons and the prospects from natality. Furthermore natality is about sponteneity, where 'freedom can only arise from something that is not the determinate product of a causal chain' (Bowring 2011: 22).

I pursue these matters in the next five chapters, where I locate the analysis mainly in England as an interesting site: in Chapter 2 I examine the ELMA field and the development of TLP in more detail and I use Arendt's analysis about lying to examine colonisation of knowledge production; in Chapter 3 I think about the potential crystallisation of totalitarian conditions through examining Arendt's analysis and using it to think through the situation in public education; in Chapter 4 I focus on the *vita activa* where I use Arendt's distinctions between labour, work and action to examine professional practice, before going on to look at the *vita contemplativa* in Chapter 5 where, in collaboration with David Hall, we examine the banality of leadership. In Chapter 6, I undertake a critical engagement with Arendt's ideas in order to examine trends in ELMA. The final short section is in common with all the books in the series and is an anotated bibliography.

As I take forward this project I am identifying with Arendt's call to engage in something that is 'very simple: it is nothing more than to think about what we are doing' (Arendt 1958: 5).

2 Hannah Arendt and the study and practice of ELMA

Introduction

ELMA is usually presented as 'speaking for itself' whereby the utterance of particular words generates common sense notions that activity associated with teaching and learning must be led, managed and administered as the prime organisational processes. Developing from and alongside ELMA is the TLP as a nationally contextualised global business regarding training, personnel recruitment and consultancy-supported organisational efficiency and effectiveness (Gunter 2012a). I intend in this chapter not only to examine how this works and why, but also to draw on and extend critiques through the use of Arendt's approach to political and historical thinking. Specifically I use Arendt's (1972) essay 'Lying in politics' as a means through which to examine globalising trends in privatisation such as the academies programme under New Labour from 2000 and the current Conservative-led coalition government from 2010. In doing this I show that TLP is a functional delivery process which enables fictions and lies to be transformed into modernisation truths, and I identify other forms of ELMA that are necessary not only to challenge the lies but also to generate alternative truths.

ELMA and social science

ELMA is concerned with the study and practice of teaching and learning, with special regard to the role of professionals, organisational structures and cultures. Consequently there are studies of schools (e.g. Richardson 1973), higher education (e.g. Fitzgerald *et al.* 2012) and local authorities (e.g. Bush and Kogan 1982); there are studies of particular roles (e.g. Lortie 2009), and of roles within organisations (e.g. Southworth 1995). Studies that examine the context in which schools and professionals are located tend to be concerned with policy and governance (e.g. Grace 1995, Saltman and Gabbard 2011), and while school-based ELMA features in such studies, the emphasis tends to be on the relationship between agency and structure within professional practice (e.g. Ball 1990, Lingard *et al.* 2003).

ELMA is a field that includes professionals, parents, children, researchers and policymakers, and hence there are debates about how best to undertake and organise teaching and learning, and how decisions are made regarding such matters. There are a number of key features regarding the development of this field:

- **The purposes of the field are not agreed, but organisational efficiency and effectiveness dominates.** For example, there have been ongoing debates about how the field is to be characterised and labelled, with shifts from educational administration to management to leadership. The rationale for these changes has tended to be driven by claims about modernisation and the need to have parity of status with the private sector (Gunter 2004). What seems to unify the field is the focus on children and their learning, but how this is engaged with varies. There are those who position themselves in a civic project and who see publicly funded education as key to developing education, securing equity and democratic development through teaching and learning (e.g. Ranson 1993). Consequently, ELMA is about and for education, and is itself educational. While there has been a tradition of linking it to professional roles and functions, the debate continues to focus on ELMA as a communal and shared concept (e.g. Foster 1986, Smyth 1989) which has a strong commitment to activism regarding radical changes and democratic inclusivity (e.g. Anderson 2009, Bogotch *et al.* 2008, Normore 2008). However, what has come to dominate is *organisational* LMA rather than *educational* LMA, where the emphasis is on the necessary processes for a functionally efficient organisation with appropriately behaved adults and children (compare Leithwood *et al.* 1999 with Lingard *et al.* 2003). So in England there are those who position themselves in regard to dismantling the civic project as a means of enabling the school as an organisation to develop as a business within the market place (e.g. Tooley 1995), and this neoliberal position is in alliance with neoconservatives who want the school to operate as a place where a traditional moral code is transmitted regarding the curriculum, behaviour and belief systems (e.g. Cox and Dyson 1968). This position within ELMA is variously entrepreneurial and moral, and has its antecedence in the Victorian headmaster tradition (Grace 1995).
- **The field has pluralistic knowledge claims and methodologies, but there are clear attempts to canonise best practice.** This is largely because it is a field rather than a discipline: the field draws on

history, political science, sociology and psychology, and as such particular theories, methodologies and methods are engaged with, synthesised and used (Gunter 2001a). The dominance of neoliberal and neoconservative purposes is based on an assumption that knowledge claims have been settled, and increasingly much of what is presented as efficient and effective school leadership is more about activity than research and theorising located in the social sciences. Indeed, there is impatience with and often downright hostility to scholarly debates and evidence. The emphasis tends to be on futuring replete with millennium imaginings based on the urgency of getting things right for the next generation. Consequently, ELMA as activity tends to be supported by belief systems about the normality of leaders, leading and leadership, and legitimised through the unreflexive acceptance of a mishmash of business thinking from Taylorism and Human Relations (see series foreword). While the Theory Movement as the search for the one best way of doing ELMA has collapsed, the idea of finding the one best approach remains seductive, and so the business model of transformational leadership has been adopted with the emphasis on the headteacher as a charismatic local leader bringing about radical change through the implementation of national reforms. Such an approach brings security as the accepted way, but also can accommodate localised pragmatism in the implementation of complex and often contradictory reforms. The challenges of rapid reform have led to the popularisation of hybrid models: instructional leadership from the US as a means of linking the headteacher directly with classroom activity; and distributed leadership (also known as 'shared' or 'total' leadership) as a means of ensuring the efficient and effective delegation of tasks and responsibility.

- Field purposes and knowledge production have been subject to the control of different communities, but the trend has been to take control from the profession and professors. In the US there has been the tradition of professorial control through the Theory Movement, but Greenfield's challenge to this was welcomed in England where the tradition has been more pragmatic (Gunter 1999, and see series foreword). The complexity of this can be illustrated with the example of field development in England. The growth of publicly funded secondary education in England from 1945 onwards generated control by the profession in schools and local authorities. The establishment of the field in higher education in England from the 1960s onwards, mainly by members of the profession relocating to universities and polytechnics, shows control by the profession in their status as professors providing professional development courses, postgraduate programmes and more recently research (Baron and Taylor 1969, Hughes 1978, Hughes *et al.* 1985). The privatisation of publicly funded education in England from the 1980s onwards challenged control by the profession and the professors, particularly as the market, with parents as consumers and private businesses as providers, grew rapidly. Specifically, governments have sought to open up education to the market place with various neoliberal projects such as site-based management within local democratic systems, and increasingly schools outside of local democracy such as academies and free schools (Gunter 2011), and to regulate schools through the curriculum, testing, codes of behaviour and performance management of the workforce. ELMA has been designed using TLP as the means by which national governments can secure the delivery of reforms locally through a leadership of schools strategy (Gunter 2012a). Governments have directly intervened in the design of leadership as an educational and professional imperative, the argument being that children's learning will be improved by efficient and effective ELMA. However, at the time this was happening Hall and Southworth (1997) argued that beyond a common sense set of beliefs that leaders, leading and leadership matters there was little substantial or independent research evidence for this. Nevertheless, policy has been conducted as if there was, where leaders have been separated out organisationally through training, pay and performance requirements, and symbolically through a cultural and media focus on particular headteachers as world-class leaders. Increasingly the label of 'principal' is being used to enable people with generic leadership skills developed in other services (public, private or voluntary) to take on the leadership role in schools. Massive investments have been made in training programmes, events and conferences, and a multi-million pound National College was set up in 2000 to determine, control and lead the field in regard to research, training and the delivery of national reforms (Gunter 2012a).

So in England ELMA is now a government-sponsored field where purposes and knowledge production are regarded as settled, knowledge claims about organisational leadership are obvious and common sense, and control is through the market which is focused on meeting professional needs by telling the profession what it needs. ELMA has been colonised, used and developed by and through the TLP as a globalised and globalising leadership industry, where members of ELMA have variously willingly and unwillingly collaborated (Gunter 2012a). The assumed political neutrality of the TLP means that products and processes have crossed political boundaries with continuities in the New Labour (1997–2010) and Conservative-led coalition (from May 2010) strategies regarding knowledge claims. However, right-wing ideology underpins the TLP where it seems that private interests have sought to retake control of and then dominate public services, and are doing this under the cloak of acting in the public interest. The system of schools funded by the public is being dismantled and privatised as a means of marketising educational products, with visible trends towards 'for profit' schooling and creating a work-ready workforce, while research shows that this is not fit for purpose and certainly does not secure equitable access and outcomes (Gunter 2011).

Thinking and acting politically and historically have a role to play in exposing this situation and in identifying alternative ways in which education can be organised and practised. In my research into knowledge production (Gunter 2012a) I have identified three main research positions on the relationship between ideas and action:

> **Government policy regimes.** I identified a New Labour Policy Regime (NLPR) between 1997 and 2010, where the government accessed and contributed to the TLP. Specifically New Labour drew on beliefs and experiences of schools to support its policies, and made mainly normative claims regarding ELMA practice. In addition, it enabled particular types of close to practice theorising (e.g. planning, teams, the development of 'can do' cultures) by contracted private consultants, professionals and researchers (e.g. Astle and Ryan 2008, DfES/PwC 2007, Leo *et al.* 2010), and some mid-range theorising on effective/ineffective and improving/failing schools, to be used (e.g. Coles and Southworth 2005). Research from school improvement and school effectiveness, hybridised through business change models and cultures, was dominant (e.g. Day *et al.* 2009, Leithwood *et al.* 2006). This activity is largely devoid of political and historical thinking, as the relationship between government and knowledge production is through a process of institutionalised governance, where government is in control (informally through people who are known and trusted, and formally through contracts) of who is allowed into policymaking and on what terms. Under what I currently call the Conservative Market Regime (CMR) from May 2010 the continued investment in the National College means that this functional and policy delivery approach to theory and theorising remains, though the increased emphasis on the market means that knowledge is valuable as a TLP commodity rather than as research-informed evidence, and debates are eschewed in favour of common sense ideology (for example, see

Gove 2010). Overall, while the issues talked about require historical and political analysis, the necessary social science scholarship to do this is largely absent.

School leadership regime (SLR). I identified that from the 1960s there has been a community based on partnerships between the profession and higher education regarding professional development, particularly through postgraduate programmes as *de facto* ELMA credentials (Gunter 1999, Gunter 2012a). This regime has been populated by school improvement and effectiveness researchers, but it is mainly a site for those who have located in the BELMAS (British Educational Leadership Management and Administration Society) network. Unlike the Government policy regimes there is research that draws on and contributes to social science theories and methodologies, and examines: (a) the biographical stories of those who work in ELMA roles (e.g. Ribbins 1997, Southworth 1995); (b) the micropolitical process of professional conduct and organisational cultures (e.g. Hoyle 1982, 1999); (c) the assumed causal connection between the elite leader and professional practice, and so is critical of the approaches to leadership as leader-centric (e.g. Gronn 2010); (d) the relationship between schools and democracy (e.g. Woods 2005); and (e) matters of diversity and in particular considers the gendered nature of school structures and cultures (e.g. Coleman 2002). Importantly, the security of this regime is problematic due to retirements and untimely deaths, but also government regimes through their engagment with the TLP have either drawn knowledge workers into exchange relations with them or towards them in expectation of such exchanges. Some knowledge workers have rejected this and moved towards social science research, where there have been more texts about leadership with a critical remit that challenges the normality of functional ELMA (e.g. Morrison 2009).

Policy research regime (PRR). I identified a research community in higher education which works with the profession in seeking to understand the relationship between ideas and action. This network variously examines particular close to practice and mid-range theories, but also engages with social science disciplines regarding the location and exercise of power in public and education policy: first, policy theorising regarding approaches to policy studies (e.g. Ball 1994, Bowe *et al.* 1992; Rizvi and Lingard 2010, Ozga 1987, Ranson 1995); second, analysis of education policy (e.g. Angus 2012, Ball 2012, Smyth 1993); third, analysis of schools and the profession (e.g. Barker 2010, Blackmore 1999, Gewirtz 2002, Gunter and

Thomson 2010, Thomson 2009); fourth, analysis of children and learning (Galton 2007, Smyth *et al.* 2008); and fifth, presentation of alternative ways in which schools and learning can develop (Fielding and Moss 2011, Thomson and Gunter 2006). Political science theories and historical thinking is evident in this research with projects that (a) relate closely to practice activity with neoliberal global trends in the markets and economy (Smyth 2011); (b) examine issues of governance and seek to contribute to theorising, e.g. debate by Ball (2008, 2009) and Goodwin (2009) on networks; (c) use theories of the state to seek to understand and explain the relationship between policy and practice (e.g. Ball 2007); and (d) use social science theories to explain the location and exercise of power (e.g. Ball 1990). Much of this research is socially critical in the sense that the aim is to use political science and historical thinking not only to problem pose regarding the field but also to reveal alternative ways in which ELMA might be thought of differently. In doing this field members have a political commitment to work against injustice and for a more just approach to public service access and experience.

This book is located in the PRR approach to the field; I intend to build on research that aims to open up the TLP to scrutiny (e.g. Ball 1995, Gunter 1997, Thrupp and Willmott 2003). Given that such accounts show a productive relationship between political theory, historical analysis and the field of critical policy studies in education, the issue that I now want to explore is what Arendt's ideas and methods can contribute.

The contribution of thinking with Arendt to ELMA

Those who research and make a contribution to ELMA position themselves differently in relation to engagement with political and historical thinking: for the PRR it is integral and for government regimes it is often used pragmatically in laminating policy, but overall it is regarded as an irrelevance. I would want to argue that the field as a whole could learn from the PRR regarding engagement with conceptual tools and methodologies from the social sciences (see Gunter 2012a). In addition to this I argue here that the field as a whole, including PRR, could learn from Arendt's approach to research and conceptualisation of issues. This is at the core of an argument that will unfold through this book, where the case is made that the major crises of our time are that the conditions of totalitarianism are central to understanding the way solutions are configured within the TLP, and following Arendt may enable crystallisation to happen through the exercise of 'good practice'.

In working on the purposes of education, and the issues that ELMA in particular focuses on, then I would want to give attention to how twentieth-century genocide broke with tradition in such a way that accepted social science methodologies and methods cannot be relied upon to generate evidential truths: 'the originality of totalitarianism is horrible, not because some new "idea" came into the world, but because its very actions constitute a break with all our traditions; they have clearly exploded our categories of political thought and our standards of moral judgment' (Arendt 1994: 310). This has implications for social science as a research practice:

> 'Normal men do not know that everything is possible', said one of the survivors of Buchenwald. Social scientists, being normal men, will have great difficulties in understanding that limitations which usually are thought to be inherent in the human condition could be transcended, that behavior patterns and motives which usually are identified, not with the psychology of some specific nation or class at some specific moment of its history, but with human psychology in general are abolished or play quite a secondary role, that objective necessities conceived as the ingredients of reality itself, adjustment to which seems a mere question of elementary sanity, could be neglected.
>
> (Arendt 1994: 241)

I argue that everything is possible in public education: the privatisation of educational services; the residualisation of the curriculum as basic work skills; and the deprofessionalisation of the workforce. Adults and children who cannot or will not operate successfully in the market place or secure philanthropic charity are superfluous and will be punished in the shift from welfare to 'prison fare' (Wacquant 2009). So researchers cannot use terminology such as educational 'leadership', 'management' and 'administration' without re-examining what the situation under scrutiny means for the exercise of power. Political and historical thinking can usefully adopt Arendt's approach to examining the meanings of such words and the relationship with practice, and think about and judge how the current situation can be examined by looking to the past to show what is new or different.

The task is to gather, record and talk through stories, and for Arendt:

> not only do stories evade theoretical abstractions, but they reconnect truth and politics by revealing multiple perspectives while remaining open and attentive to the unexpected, the unpredictability and contingency of action, the possibility of change and new beginnings, which is at the heart of what politics is about. In doing so, stories untimately

reconfigure the sphere of politics as an open plane of horizontal connections, wherein the revolution can once again be re-imagined.

(Tamboukou 2012: 11)

So for the historical and political thinker the aim is to seek understanding rather than just gather evidence:

> Understanding, as distinguished from having correct information and scientific knowledge, is a complicated process which never produces unequivocal results. It is an unending activity by which, in constant change and variation, we come to terms with and reconcile ourselves to reality, that is, try to be at home in the world.
>
> (Arendt 1994: 307–308)

For example, much of what is presented in the debates about what makes leadership distinct from management and administration tends to focus on definitions developed within and for the TLP (see Gunter 2001a). So understanding is limited to ways of thinking, talking and working in the organisation (e.g. leadership is about pathfinding and management is about pathfollowing). This seems to be innocent enough, particularly as it could be both inspiring and helpful: a person engages with the metaphor of the pathway and sees what they need to do differently, and can be provided with the means by which to do this (leadership can use a SWOT analysis, and management can use planning). But this assumes that business models can be transferred without damaging 'public', 'education' and 'system' within the public education system. However when, for example, team working is promoted as the best way of organising activity then much of what is presented to the educational professional is disconnected from professional values, histories and politics (see Gunter 1997). Specifically, the case can be made that the process of team work, devoid of educational values, knowledge and practices, disconnects the teacher from the politics of public education. Working in a team is common sense good practice, and when this is combined with the standards agenda regarding personal responsibility for targets and data then teachers are made so busy that they are blinkered to the dismantling of public education. While teams are presented as energetic, 'can do' and enable accountability, I would want to make the case that team working is a hollow process currently filled with neoliberal and neoconservative agendas. Specifically, such teams position children as data producers and teachers as data collectors, where the latter are redesigned as a generic, flexible, deployable and removable workforce.

Arendt's approach is helpful because she argues for distinctions, and so false ones in regard to administration, management and leadership can be revealed. Using her ideas to think about this one issue shows the limited understanding that the government regimes have operated within. Much of the ELMA work on leadership and associated processes such as team working is based on what Arendt (1994) calls 'preliminary understanding' or a basic grasp of a situation, and what is needed is what she calls a 'true understanding' based on getting underneath 'the judgments and prejudices which preceded and guided the strictly scientific inquiry. The sciences can only illuminate, but neither prove or disprove, the uncritical preliminary understanding from which they start' (Arendt 1994: 311). By beginning on the basis that the distinctions between leadership and management and administration can only be from TLP knowledge claims then the marginalisation of research on this in education (e.g. Hodgkinson 1983) can be understood. So in my investigations I need to examine the starting assumptions of research and practice, and following Arendt, I should engage in 'thinking without a banister' (Canovan 1995: 6, Miller 1995: unpaged). Climbing the stairs of thinking and understanding has nothing to hold on to as all previous steps should be scrutinised:

> when she sets off, then, to think 'without a banister' to hold on to, reflecting freely upon events, and writing in a way that records trains of thought instead of presenting a theory, her readers are naturally led to expect that her thoughts will not be particularly consistent, and will certainly not in any way resemble a system.
>
> (Canovan 1995: 6)

Instead of imposing pre-determined categories on events, Canovan (1995) argues that Arendt's work is like a spider's web where there are interconnections: 'one cannot understand one part of her thought unless one is aware of its connections with all the rest' (ibid.: 6).

The contribution of Arendt's historical and political thinking to ELMA

Arendt's approach eschews linear analysis as if events were inevitable, and instead she regarded an event as a break that required detailed analysis. Here I intend experimenting with this by using Arendt's (1972) work 'Lying in politics' to think about the academies programme in England (Gunter 2011). By identifying a lie I mean a deliberate falsification of a case in order to mislead the thinking and debate of others, and this is different from politicking based on fabrications (e.g. selecting and interpreting, mythmaking), briefing for or against (e.g. image creation and leaking of information regarding a person/group), spin (e.g. managing information to create a positive story), burying bad news (e.g. releasing statistics or a change in policy at a time when public attention is distracted by a major event) and damage limitation (e.g. rescuing image and credibility).

In 2000 the then New Labour government set up in England what it called 'independent state schools' funded by government and private sponsors, and autonomous from local authority planning and accountability (Blunkett 2000). The aim was to convert existing 'failing' secondary schools, originally in cities, into schools outside of local planning and democratic control based on claims to improve student outcomes through a combination of private interests, organisational leadership, additional investment and release from the requirements of the national curriculum. The programme has been expanded under the Conservative-led coalition from May 2010 by opening it to all schools, including primary schools and outstanding secondaries. The academies programme is highly controversial, and my approach here begins with three stories which illuminate political and historical lies (along with illustrations of fabrications, spin etc.).

Story 1

Northern (2011: 33) has reported that academies are investing in large senior leadership teams on large salaries rather than in teaching and learning:

> Senior positions advertised in the past few weeks include that of executive director of the 1,300-pupil New Charter Academy in Tameside. In return for a six-figure salary, the successful applicant is to inspire an executive team of four, including an academy director and a leadership team of 16. In Kent, the 1,600-pupil Business Academy, Bexley, is offering to pay an assistant head up to £61,000 to bolster its leadership team of chief executive, executive principal (both earning in excess of £120k) and two headteachers plus assorted deputy and assistant heads. In Norfolk, the 1,300-pupil Thetford Academy is advertising for two vice-principals on salaries of up to £74,000 to joint its leadership team of 24.

Such a development is based on lies with large doses of spin: that having people who are trained and identified as leaders, doing leading and exercising leadership, and who operate as a team separate from the rest of the 'workforce', will improve teaching and learning. At best the evidence is minimal and patchy, and the main meta-analysis projects (e.g. Hallinger and Heck 1996), including government-funded reports (e.g. Leithwood *et al.* 2006), show that the most important people in teaching and learning are teachers and they tend to mediate the impact of senior leaders. The evidence on academies shows that there is no 'Academy Effect' (PwC 2008) and in the main they tend to do the same as their predecessor schools, and if they are doing better it is because they are teaching different types of children and have distorted the curriculum in order to generate positive data (see Gunter 2011, Wrigley 2012).

The academies are under huge pressure to be seen to be successful, and so the emphasis has been on data generation and positive stories. By connecting the academies programme and the approach to ELMA back to other experiments (e.g. city technology colleges) and the 1988 Education Reform Act, which created schools as small businesses within a market, then a 'true understanding' can develop regarding the separation of an elite cadre of leaders disconnected from teaching and learning as a means of breaking the professional power of teachers and installing private sector values and processes. Professional identity has been re-designed around comparison and equivalence with private sector entre-preneurs (Forde *et al.* 2000), and this makes ELMA an attractive career opportunity for non-education and non-public service leaders. By connecting this further back through the work of Grace (1995) then the current entrepreneurial and chief executive role of the headteacher can be linked to the nineteenth-century public school headmaster, and the role of the head as leading professional which grew in the immediate post-World War Two era can be recognised as having been marginalised. The frustration by successive governments has been that positioning by professionals has varied: there are enthusiastic collaborators, ambivalent implementers and opponents (Gunter and Forrester 2009), and so the penetration of the fabrications remains problematic because some profes-sionals not only recognise what is going on but answer back (e.g. Arrowsmith 2001). However, even though experiments fail, and imperti-nent questions can be asked (e.g. if teachers have the most impact on learning then why has all this economic, cultural and symbolic investment gone into headteachers?), the actual lie (with myths and imaginings of a 'better' education system) does create the cultures and practices that make people ready to accept or at least not challenge the next batch of policy narratives. If a teacher is told throughout their career that teachers are failing children and that they need to do things differently (or they face public humiliation and loss of their job) then one response is to leave (and there have been shortages as a result; see Gunter 2005) or comply (see Yarker 2005).

Story 2

Davis (2012: 13) has reported a speech by Michael Gove (2012), the Secretary of State, where he attacks those he identifies as opponents of the academies programme:

> Mr Gove said the Government would press on with plans to turn 200 of the worst-performing primary schools into academies, despite some local authorities being obstructive. He said 'the same ideologues who are happy with failure – the enemies of promise – also say you can't get the same results in the inner cities as the leafy suburbs, so it's wrong to stigmatise these schools . . . Government figures show that three out of five "outstanding" secondary schools have applied to convert to academy status, and around one in three pupils in state secondary schools now attends an academy.' Criticising the anti-academies campaign, Mr Gove said: 'futures are being blighted. Horizons are being limited. Generations of children are being let down. And yet the response of those "campaigners" to an attempt to rescue the situation is "hands off". It's the same old ideologues pushing the same old ideology of failure and mediocrity . . . Change is coming. And to those who want to get in the way, I have just two words: hands off.'

The speech is based on: first, fabrications that those who oppose academies are automatically in support of failure; second, spin in which Gove (2012) talks about opponents as 'they' so that there is a spectre of destructive revolutionaries haunting this policy; and third a lie about the evidence for the setting up and expansion of the programme:

> The Academies programme is not about ideology. It's an evidence-based, practical solution built on by successive governments – both Labour and Conservative. The new ideologues are the enemies of reform, the ones who put doctrine ahead of pupils' interests. Every step of the way, they have sought to discredit our policies, calling them divisive, destructive, ineffective, unpopular, unworkable – even 'a crime against humanity'.
>
> (Gove 2012: unpaged)

Research shows that there was no evidence in 2000 for the academies programme to be launched. There was a sense that something radical had to be done, and there were incomplete experiments in England such as the city technology colleges and inconclusive evidence from the US regarding charter schools. Research that tracked the academies programme shows that there was no evidence regarding claims about teaching and learning for continuing with or expanding the programme (Gunter 2011). Indeed, those who benefited from the original city academies policy, with its emphasis on private sponsors receiving public sector assets in return for investing in schools, were opposed to the New Labour shift towards local authorities and schools being sponsors (see Gunter 2011). The Gove expansion of the academies programme to include primary schools and outstanding secondary schools is not based on a complete or robust evidence base but a 'mythbuster' (DfE 2010) document which has selected gobbets of information to support the policy. Importantly, what is 'failing' and what is 'satisfactory' has been recalibrated several times, and in ways that catch out professionals and children as they fall below the new benchmark. In this way 'failing' primary schools are in the same situation as second-aries were in 2000 when the removal from local authority control was believed to be necessary to improve education, yet outstanding secondary schools have clearly been successful under local authority control and so the need to convert remains a puzzle. It seems that the underlying lie is about local authorities failing schools and children, which has its origins in neoliberal concerns that local co-ordinated planning of provision is denying market penetration. There is an ideological opposition to local democracy which means that privatisation and dismantling was preferred over reform and civic renewal. Local democracy is based on a potential 'rival' mandate which challenges the UK government mandate in England, and local democracy operates on communal services rather than on compe-tition. Low turn out rates at local elections can be contrasted unfavourably with the data, suggesting popularity of the new schools for parents and professionals, and yet applications for children to attend an academy or for a school to convert should not be confused with endorsement and support. Strategising in a market place does not mean that parents and professionals support markets (see Newman and Clarke 2009), or do not value local democracy, or that they will not, as the Anti Academies Alliance campaigns have shown, oppose the changes.

Story 3

Boffey (2012: 10) reports on resistance to the academies programme:

> Gove wants to force Downhills, which inspectors last year put under notice to improve its performance, to accept that it will become an academy by the end of the month or face the dissolution of its governing body. The move is part of a government drive to turn 200 under-performing primary schools into academies, funded by the state but

run by sponsors which are often private companies, trusts, charities or religious organisations. However, Gove has been frustrated by parents and governors at some schools, including those at Downhills, who have rebelled against the changes. Last week, the minister described campaigners at the school fighting his academies programme as 'ideologues' who were putting 'doctrine ahead of pupils' interests' by preventing him from tackling failure. However, parents and governors at Downhills believe they have a strong case against the government. They say drastic steps have been taken to lift standards and a monitoring visit by inspectors last September found a 'clear trend of improvement'.

Such a development is based on the lies illuminated by Stories 1 and 2, and exposes the lie that neoliberal and neoconservative reforms have been based on, namely that reform through choice will benefit parents, children and communities, and that ELMA can deliver high-quality education. Normative claims about handing over decisions to parents and communities through market-based choice is underpinned by influential texts, such as Bobbitt's (2002) *The Shield of Achilles*, where he argues that the nation state based on security and welfare is no longer appropriate and is being replaced by the market state:

> with its scepticism about government and its compact with individual choice, the prospect of turning over education to parents is welcomed enthusiastically. Voucher systems – which effectively use the state as a tuition collector, rebating the collected fees to private and public schools that are chosen by parents – are likely to become the standard, not the exceptional, means of school selection . . . The voucher scheme is precisely the sort of expansion of opportunity the market-state undertakes to provide: more options, less coercion by law.
>
> (Bobbitt 2003: 242)

No doubt Bobbitt would argue that the problem with cases such as Downhills is that Gove is involved at all. Certainly the parents and communities around this school have identified that they are being denied a citizenship choice through the ballot box, and are concerned that the opportunities to exercise this choice are being curtailed through the ending of local authority control (Boffey 2012). If I think politically and historically then I know that successive governments which have claimed the value of rolling back the state and opening up public services to private providers have at the same time given secretaries of state additional powers to make interventions under the banner of increasing parental and community choice. So while educational professionals have been told that they are being freed up to exercise ELMA in ways that will secure high standards, in reality they are denied a strategic role in favour of localised tactical delivery of reforms which are externally determined. While there has been rhetoric about improved professional status (DfEE 1998), in reality professionals face continued deprofessionalisation through remodelling where non-teaching qualified people are brought in to do a teacher's job and schools outside of local authority control are allowed to suspend national terms and conditions of service (Butt and Gunter 2007).

The opportunity to make choices through the ballot box has been restricted. So while grant maintained status from 1988 was awarded based on a local ballot, this was not offered to communities in regard to the academies programme. Local politics in regard to this programme has been denied in ways that should be of concern to democrats (see Barker 2010, Elliott 2011, Hatcher 2011). Instead the mandate has been used to favour and bolster private and powerful elite interests (Woods *et al.* 2007) in ways that challenge democratic integrity (Beckett 2007), and choice is through the staking of economic power through purchasing an education (e.g. sponsors purchasing the education of other people's children through what is called 'philanthropy') rather than through democratic debate and shared participation in local government systems. The irony is that parents and communities have to be told the error of their ways and thinking, and have to be relocated in a market so that they can exercise the right type of choice.

Arendt (1972) is helpful in enabling the field to think about the relationship between ELMA and the TLP raised by these three stories. She wrote her essay 'Lying in politics' (Arendt 1972) in response to the Pentagon Papers published in 1968. She exposed 'aspects of deception, self-deception, image-making, ideologizing, and defactualization' (ibid.: 44) in relation to the Vietnam War. Specifically the Pentagon Papers made transparent the bombing and killing of non-combatants, but also showed 'beyond doubt and in tedious repetition that this not very honorable and not very rational enterprise was exclusively guided by the needs of a superpower to create for itself an *image* which would *convince* the world that it was indeed "the mightiest power on earth" ' (Arendt 2003: 263). So successive governments in England have lied and invested in the TLP in order to promote and defend status as a serious player in a global economy, and so they must be seen to be doing something to make changes in order to bring about a better education system, particularly as a result of international test results. For Arendt (1972) the 'ability to lie' is about changing facts based on a use of imagination or how 'things might well be different from what they actually are' (ibid.: 5). For example, in 1997 the then New

Labour government said in support of its interventions into the redesign of professional practice that: 'Good heads can transform a school; poor heads can block progress and achievement' (DfEE 1997: 46). In addition to the point already made about the limited evidence, it is also the case that the 'goodness' and 'poorness' of a head can be successfully identified and transmitted, and that people are in a context where that preferred and calculated 'goodness' can be demonstrated and that people go into work everyday to demonstrate 'poorness'. What is interesting about lies, fabrications and spin is that they can be presented as plausible because the liar knows the audience, and can be shown for what they are through the sheer weight of evidence or the 'immensity of factuality' (Arendt 1972: 7). Consequently my work on the development of the field (Gunter 1999, 2001a), with a specific focus on knowledge production (Gunter 2012a), has exposed the processes used to popularise common sense beliefs as 'scientific' lies that the TLP can sell.

Arendt (1972) enhances this analysis by describing and explaining two modern types of lying: first, 'the apparent innocuous one of the public-relations managers in government who learned their trade from the inventiveness of Madison Avenue' (Arendt 1972: 7–8). Notably she identifies the use of advertising to sell a way of life, so that the consumer will buy into it. The setting up of the National College for School Leadership was not based on a secure evidence base but a combination of common sense beliefs, private sector models and the imagination of the school as a successful firm, where the best form of professional practice was advertised as leadership (see Hopkins 2001). This message was relentless and ritualistic, where the idea of not being a leader and not accepting followership increasingly became unthinkable.

The second type of lying is by 'professional problem solvers' who 'were drawn into government from the universities and the various think tanks, some of them equipped with game theories and systems analyses, thus prepared, as they thought, to solve all the "problems" of foreign policy' (Arendt 1972: 9–10). My research on the leadership field shows resonance with Arendt's analysis that they engaged 'for many years in the game of deceptions and falsehoods . . . they lied perhaps out of a mistaken patriotism' (Arendt 1972: 10–11). It seems to me that the professional problem solvers handled the emphasis on elite adults through a fabricated commitment to children and their learning – they pursued the idea that ELMA was the most important means of improving teaching and learning. Buying into the TLP ensured that teaching and learning were turned into products to be delivered to a quiescent student population who would benefit by being trained in the skills and behaviours necessary for the workplace. Once inside Whitehall (or its arm's length bodies, e.g. the

National College) they overtly took on the zealous reforming culture, and as such 'the problem solvers, who lost their minds because they trusted the calculating powers of their brains at the expense of the mind's capacity for experience and its ability to learn from it' (Arendt 1972: 39).

While there is evidence that people disagreed with the emphasis on the charismatic transformational leader, who could turn a school around and secure higher test results, they tended to moderate what was being proposed and/or wait for the opportunity to renegotiate the agenda, thus ensuring that their insider status was not threatened. Indeed, the problem solvers 'believed in methods but not in "world views," which, incidentally, is the reason they could be trusted' (Arendt 1972: 40). They presented themselves as politically neutral, and so problem solvers who worked with Conservative (1979–1997) and New Labour (1997–2010) governments focused on delivery rather than on debates about educational purposes. Finally, Arendt (1972: 11) notes that:

> they were eager to find formulas, preferably expressed in a pseudo-mathematical language, that would unify the most disparate phenomena with which reality presented to them; that is, they were eager to discover *laws* by which to explain and predict political and historical facts as though they were as necessary, and thus as reliable, as the physicists once believed natural phenomena to be.

My own research shows that the dominance of school improvement and school effectiveness knowledge production in education policymaking assumed the school is a unitary organisation where the implementation of the right type of conditions combined with methods of measuring impact and value added calculations could provide a modern take on the Theory Movement (Gunter 2012a). Specifically that the technical laws of improvement and efficiency could be secured through the installation of trained and co-opted leaders who had been given the knowledge and know how about how to dismantle public education under the cloak of making a difference to children's learning. While debates have taken place regarding the different impacts on learning outcomes of the school and the wider social and economic issues, the emphasis in SESI (School Effectiveness and School Improvement) on working with governments on delivering a reform agenda (e.g. Reynolds *et al.* 1996) means that important issues have not received attention (see Slee *et al.* 1998). So scholarly work on the organisational realities for teachers (e.g. Smyth and McInerney 2007), children (e.g. Fielding 2006, Smyth *et al.* 2004), headteachers (e.g. Barker 1999) and schools (Gewirtz 2002) interconnects with what Arendt (1972) calls 'world views' or the bigger picture.

Ravitch (2010a) has exposed the lies within reforms that she admits she used to be complicit with: that effective teachers who deliver the right type of test data are more effective than teachers who 'love' their subject and who work with children in developing understandings; and that closing a school, or schools creaming off particular categories of children that lead to school closure, will benefit communities:

> Our schools will not improve if we entrust them to the magical powers of the market. Markets have winners and losers. Choice may lead to better outcomes or to worse outcomes. Letting a thousand flowers bloom does not guarantee a garden full of flowers. If the garden is untended, unsupervised and unregulated, it is likely to become overgrown with weeds. Our goal must be to establish school systems that foster academic excellence in every school and every neighborhood.
>
> (Ravitch 2010a: 227)

The end of the first decade of the twenty-first century also brought damning evidence about the consequences of markets through the focus on equity. Wilkinson and Pickett (2009) used data to show that the arguments that had been made about the consequences of choice and competition had substance in ways that the neoliberals and neoconservatives, no matter how hard they tried, could not successfully brief against. The equity gap relating to the proven link between socio-economic advantage and educational success remains stubborn, where aspirational dispositions are directly related to strategising within the family (Reay *et al.* 2005). There are serious consequences of this, as Judt (2010) eloquently articulates:

> The result is an eviscerated society. From the point of view of the person at the bottom – seeking unemployment pay, medical attention, social benefits or other officially mandated services – it is no longer the state, the administration or the government that he or she instinctively turns to. The service or benefit in question is now often 'delivered' by a private intermediary. As a consequence, the thick mesh of social interactions and public goods has been reduced to a minimum, with nothing except authority and obedience binding the citizen to the state. This reduction of 'society' to a thin membrane of interactions between private individuals is presented today as the ambition of libertarians and free marketers. But we should never forget that it was first and above all the dream of Jacobins, Bolsheviks and Nazis: if there is nothing that binds us together as a community or society, then we are utterly dependent upon the state. Governments that are too weak or discredited to act through their citizens are more likely to seek their

ends by other means: by exhorting, cajoling, threatening and ultimately coercing people to obey them. The loss of social purpose articulated through public services actually *increases* the unrestrained powers
of the over-mighty state.

(Judt 2010: 118–119, emphasis in orginal)

This helps to explain the lying within the academies programme. There is
no space to debate, and the imposition of individualised consumer choices
is demonstrating totalitarian tendencies. The three stories from the academies programme illuminate this: Story 1 shows the promotion of ELMA
as a means to deliver high-quality teaching and learning, but in reality it
is about gaining advantage in the employment market through delivering
marketable products; Story 2 shows the promotion of ELMA as a form of
'doing as you are told' where critique is conflated with opposition, and
democratic renewal is sacrificed at the altar of delivery; and Story 3 gives a
glimpse of overt 'exhorting, cajoling, threatening . . . (and) . . . coercing
people to obey them' (Judt 2010: 119), and we must not forget the covert
influence of this on successful community schools to comply with marketisation. While those who hold ELMA posts are busy with TLP tasks such
as bidding for resources, counting test results, filling in forms and giving
inspirational talks to keep children and parents on board, the relationship
between the individual and the public domain is being changed in such
as way as to potentially deny humanity. Those who hold ELMA posts
have been trained not to recognise this, or are too exhausted or fearful
to do anything about it. The world of teachers such as Mrs Ratliff
(Ravitch 2010a) and Bob Hewitt (Gunter 2005), and headteachers such as
Bernard Barker (1999) and David Winkley (2002), seems to be not only
unmodern but positively dangerous. It is to this that I now turn, as I use
Arendt's work to think historically and politically about the crystallisation
of totalitarian conditions within public education.

3 Using Arendt to think about ELMA

Politics and totalitarianism

Introduction

Drawing mainly on *The Origins of Totalitarianism*, this chapter will examine Arendt's claims about plurality and exchange of ideas, and the relationship with freedom. Specifically I engage with the conditions in which totalitarianism develops, and it will be argued that the colonisation of professional practice through the TLP is an illuminative example of such conditions. In doing this I will examine the conditions in which ELMA has been designed, constructed and delivered to the profession. I will use Arendt's historical and political thinking as a means of refusing 'monocausal explanations' and as such 'create an understanding of the paths toward totalitarian domination and its novel crimes' (Jalušič 2007: 148). In approaching this here, and in the chapters that follow, I put the Arendtian analysis of a grave period in history for humanity alongside what is happening currently in public services education. In doing so I recognise distinctions but in using her methodologies to think with I expose similarities that need our responsible and serious attention. Notably I do this by examining a complex, multi-layered and shifting situation, which is stabilised in ways that are deemed normal and normalising.

Education, education, education

Canovan (1995: 1) contends that 'Hannah Arendt is one of the great outsiders of twentieth-century political thought, at once strikingly original and disturbingly unorthodox'. This description can be used to characterise her particular contribution to educational issues, where there are two key essays: 'Reflections on Little Rock' (Arendt 2003) and 'The crisis in education' (Arendt 2006a). Her originality is located in how she addresses major political issues through focusing on an event or situation in education, and her unorthodoxy is through how she confronts these matters in ways that speak about and speak for what might be considered by some to be unspeakable.

In 'Reflections on Little Rock' Arendt uses the Supreme Court decision to desegregate schools to raise questions about the constitution and about the positioning of children: 'to start desegregation in education and in schools had not only, and very unfairly, shifted the burden of responsibility from the shoulders of adults to those of children' (Arendt 2003: 194). What is illustrated in this essay is how the political and historical need to be rehabilitated as the means to handle contemporary problems: 'the color question was created by the one great crime in America's history and is soluble only within the political and historical framework of the Republic' (Arendt 2003: 198). Within this are concerns about the border between the private and the public, and she argues in favour of 'the rights of parents to decide such matters for their children until they are grown-ups are challenged only by dictatorships' (Arendt 2003: 195). She reproduces and focuses on a picture that shows Elizabeth Eckford coming home from an integrated school, and how she was surrounded by white children and 'protected by a white friend of her father' (p193). She asks questions about what it means to be a child in this situation and what parents think about how their child is being used politically and historically (see Duarte 2010a).

In 'The crisis in education' Arendt (2006a) identifies the problem of standards in schools to raise questions about the issue of responsibility. She identifies how progressive methods have handed over the responsibility for learning to children with two consequences, first, the connection between adult and child is broken; and second, that children become governed by a peer group that is 'more tyrannical than the severest authority of an individual person can ever be' (Arendt 2006a: 178). She also raises questions about the changes to training, where teaching has been transformed into facilitation and so the teacher does not have the authority of knowledge. For Arendt (2006a) educators have to take responsibility for enabling children to enter the world, a world they as educators will not have created and may not approve of. This manifests itself as authority: 'the teacher's qualification consists in knowing the world and being able to instruct others about it, but his authority rests on his assumption of responsibility for that world' (Arendt 2006a: 186). So again Arendt is examining the borders between adults and children, private and public, and she does so through asserting the political over the social:

> What concerns us all and cannot therefore be turned over to the special science of pedagogy is the relation between grownups and children in general or, putting it in even more general and exact terms, our

attitude toward the fact of natality: the fact that we have all come into the world by being born and that this world is constantly renewed through birth. Education is the point at which we decide whether we love the world enough to assume responsibility for it and by the same token save it from that ruin which, except for renewal, except for the coming of the new and young, would be inevitable. And education, too, is where we decide whether we love our children enough not to expel them from our world and leave them to their own devices, nor to strike from their hands their chance of undertaking something new, something unforeseen by us, but to prepare them in advance for the task of renewing a common world.

(Arendt 2006a: 193)

Arendt's (2006a) core argument is that children need to be protected within the family but at the same time the world needs protection from the potential instability of these new lives entering it and making demands for change.

Gordon (2001b: 1) notes that 'very little has been written on the educational implications of Arendt's ideas', but she inspires intellectual work within education (e.g. Giroux 2011), and there is debate in the US (e.g. Gordon 2001a, Higgins 2010) and a growing recognition in the UK (e.g. Biesta 2010) that Arendt speaks to contemporary concerns and can help thinking about serious matters. Her work is regarded as controversial, indeed offensive to some (see Benhabib 2000), but it is argued that 'Little Rock' generated thinking about how students are positioned (Duarte 2010a), and 'The crisis in education' about how the curriculum is experienced (Levinson 2010). Both of these essays illuminate Arendt's methodology:

our own study of her thought involves a double movement, back to the roots of her thinking so that we can understand her, but then forward again to see what we can learn from her. We will not understand her if we are unaware of the interconnection of her thought, but we need not suppose that her importance as a political thinker depends upon the acceptance of her story of modernity.

(Canovan 1995: 280)

Such an engagement means that I and others can examine contemporary events and relate them to the bigger picture of political and historical developments. For example, Ravitch (2010b), in reviewing the film *Waiting for 'Superman'*, examines what she calls the 'myth of charter schools'. The film is about how five children enter a lottery for a place in a charter school, and in Arendtian terms they have to resolve political issues:

In the final moments of *Waiting for 'Superman,'* the children and their parents assemble in auditoriums in New York City, Washington, D.C., Los Angeles, and Silicon Valley, waiting nervously to see if they will win the lottery. As the camera pans the room, you see tears rolling down the cheeks of children and adults alike, all their hopes focused on a listing of numbers or names. Many people react to the scene with their own tears, sad for the children who lose. I had a different reaction. First, I thought to myself that the charter operators were cynically using children as political pawns in their own campaign to promote their cause . . . Second, I felt an immense sense of gratitude to the much-maligned American public education system, where no one has to win a lottery to gain admission.

(Ravitch 2010b: 4)

Just as Arendt used events in education to speak about wider issues of the state, public policy and education, then Ravitch's (2010b) analysis of children's lives being determined by a lottery is concerned with the condition of the polity. Specifically how plurality in ideas and debates about education is being undermined, indeed ridiculed, as illustrated in the relentless onslaught against professionals taking responsibility for public education. For Arendt (2006a: 171) 'a crisis becomes a disaster only when we respond to it with preformed judgements, that is, with prejudices. Such an attitude not only sharpens the crisis but makes us forfeit the experience of reality and the opportunity for reflection it provides.' It seems that the ideological drive for markets to enter public services, such as education, means that there are 'prejudices' in favour of neoliberal and neoconservative solutions. Ravitch (along with other writers, e.g. Apple 2010) has exposed the problematics of privatisation, and provided examples of socially just democratic alternatives in ways that show the importance of Arendt's 'thinking without a banister' (see Chapter 2) as a means of understanding the particular event in question and how it relates to a wider political and historical analysis.

Nevertheless, as noted, Arendt's judgements about events and crises have made research both creative and difficult for researchers to use in their thinking and analysis in education. So there are positive aspects to thinking historically and politically with Arendt, for example Gordon (2001b: 2) argues that she 'offers a unique voice that can enhance the critical tradition's call for transforming education so that it can foster the values of democratic citizenship and social practice.' But there are concerns that Arendt is too conservative in how she addresses the positioning of children and parents, and in her arguments against the social. On balance, those who have confronted Arendt and education have found her methodology to be more helpful than limiting, and in particular radical educators claim to have been able to think productively about educational purposes and practices. Two examples here will suffice. There is evidence that using her essays on educational issues with students in the classroom has generated learning opportunities about identity. For example, Lane (2001: 171) reports that 'what my students from such varied backgrounds have compellingly demonstrated to me . . . is that it is precisely the most difficult and troubling aspects of her thought that address their deepest concerns about democratic possibilities in an increasingly multicultural world.' In the same collection Curtis (2001) shows how Arendt's arguments for plurality mean that identity is not given but is challenged, and how multiculturalism is important 'because of the way it illuminates and gives voice to the lives and perspectives of the formerly unseen and disregarded' (Curtis 2001: 148).

A second example focuses on teachers and teaching, where Gordon (2001c) argues that Arendt is conservative in how she wants to protect children rather than turn the clock back to another age. It is argued that what pulls Arendt away from anachronistic accounts, in ways that enable progressive educators to engage, is her position on politics through natality or the capacity of human beings to bring something new into the world by virtue of being born: 'natality is both what motivates political action and what mitigates against our actions having the intended effect' (Levinson 2001: 13). So the role of the teacher is to present the various understandings of the world: 'the point of this exposure to the world as it is is not to fix the world, but to motivate our students to imagine new possibilities for the future' (Levinson 2001: 20). What this means is that 'educators should expose students to those ideas and values that, though they have undergone change, have survived in a different form and can be used to interrupt, critique, and transform the present' (Gordon 2001c: 50). Arendt (2006a: 174) argues that natality is the 'essence of education', and so there is a need to educate new people born into the world but at the same time we should not prevent them from renewing the world. Central to this is how politics is understood and practised in a pluralistic way.

The politics of totalitarianism

Canovan (1995) argues that Arendt worked on the rehabilitation of politics at a time when social and economic concerns dominated. So her thinking is less about the tensions between welfare investment and market choice, and more about how to think and act politically through the pluralism of natality. Arendt (1958) argues that what is needed are places where people can be separate but at the same time connected, like sitting at a table, and: 'when this in-between world is destroyed, people find themselves pressed together so tightly that both self and world lose their integrity, and a lonely indifference to public life becomes the norm' (Bowring 2011: 3). In presenting her analysis of political action she drew inspiration from ancient city states (Arendt 2006a), but specifically she focused on the story of the American Revolution because:

> this revolution did not break out but was made by men in common deliberation and on the strength of mutual pledges. The principle which came to light during those fateful years when the foundations were laid – not by strength of one architect but by the combined power of the many – was the interconnected principle of mutual promise and common deliberation.
>
> (Arendt 2006a: 206)

For Arendt the opportunity for space and deliberation was through the council system (Young-Bruehl 1982), and Schell (2006) argues that what is central to *On Revolution* (Arendt 2006b) is the Mayflower compact:

> Here is no terror or domination of any kind. Instead a few dozen men approaching a wilderness 'covenant and combine' themselves into a 'Civil body Politik' . . . their action affirms their 'plurality' which . . . is the necessary and sufficient aspect of human life for all political activity. Not only politics generally, but political power specifically is generated by such non-violent, positive participation, or 'action in concert'.
>
> (Schell 2006: xv)

What seems to be important in her analysis is the 'abolition of sovereignty' as a form of tyranny (Young-Bruehl 1982: xxxiii–xxxiv, citing Kohn), and so the emphasis is on the localised approach to ideas, debate and decision-making: 'authentic political thought necessarily arose, she believed, out of real political events, and had to be rethought in response to them' (Canovan 1995: 5). Consequently, the responsibility she had identified in her two essays on education was central to her analysis of political life: people have to face their obligations rather than accept the inevitability of events or escape into 'private or collective fantasies' (Canovan 1995: 11).

What seems to emerge from Arendt's confrontation with American life, such as education, is a concern with a loss of memory about the origins and originality of the US constitution, and the dangers that this generates:

> we can see that her thinking moves within the framework of a contrast between two alternative political responses to the predicament of

modern humanity. On the one hand, adopting a tactic of which totalitarianism was the extreme form, human beings can maximise their power and minimise their responsibility by pretending not to be human, that is, not be plural and free: they can side with inhuman forces, make themselves and others into members of an animal species, submerge their capacity for thought in the relentless automatism of single-track logic. Alternatively, they can face up to and accept the implications of their humanity, which means accepting their plurality, their freedom to act and to think, and their joint responsibility to establish a world between them, to set limits to the forces of nature and to bestow rights upon one another. As we shall see, Arendt's mature political thought flows directly from these preoccupations.

(Canovan 1995: 62)

Analysts have recognised that the American experiment had not lived up to expectations (see Arendt 1970) 'precisely because it failed to preserve the participatory democracy of the ward system and the strength of local government as proposed by a figure such as Thomas Jefferson' (King 2011: 32). It seems that the purpose of the state became one of security rather than pluralism, and those who use Arendt to think about the nation state recognise that flaws in this conceptualisation enabled politics to be replaced by markets and consumer exchange (see Baum *et al.* 2011, Butler and Spivak 2010). Ultimately, western traditions in political thinking captured the US culture, where more emphasis is traditionally put on contemplation rather than action:

> contemplatives want to control or eliminate the uncontrolled, unpredictable realm of action and speech, the political realm. Under the influence of this prejudice, the word politics, which for Arendt refers to human beings acting – discoursing, persuading, deciding on specific deeds, doing them – in the public realm, came to refer to the rulership of one or more human beings over others.

(Young-Bruehl 2006: 83)

The danger is, and the twentieth century presents some extraordinary, terrible cases, for politics to actually disappear (Young-Bruehl 1982). The argument is that:

> totalitarianism, a novelty among forms of government, is not, like tyranny, the atrophy of politics; it is the radical elimination of politics brought about by the methodical elimination of the very humanity of

first a selected group and eventually any group, by making humans superfluous as human beings. Such is totalitarianism's 'radical evil'.

(Arendt, cited in Young-Bruehl 1982: xvii)

By rendering people to be superfluous, then, people were denied the right to have rights. This is core to understanding Arendt's thinking, and her work in *On Totalitarianism* enables analysis about the conditions in which it develops and flourishes.

Arendt (2009) identifies four features of totalitarianism: ideology, total terror, destruction of human bonds and bureaucracy.

Ideology

Arendt (2009) distinguishes that totalitarianism is based on 'an entirely new and unprecedented concept of power' (p417); it is not so much about structures and systems but actions based on an 'unwavering faith in an ideological fictitious world' (p417–418). Such fictions were attractive, and there are two features: the first is how Arendt (2009) thought historically about Nazism and Stalinism by relating contemporary events with historical antecendence, notably the relationship between imperialism and totalitarianism:

> This process of never-ending accumulation of power necessary for the protection of a never-ending accumulation of capital determined the 'progressive' ideology of the late nineteenth century and foreshadowed the rise of imperialism. Not the naïve delusion of a limitless growth of property, but the realization that power accumulation was the only guarantee for the stability of so-called economic laws, made progress irresistible.

> (Arendt 2009: 143)

Specifically she identified the importance of how the bourgeoisie worked for markets, capital accumulation and political emancipation, and how they staked their wealth and political power with a particular party or movement, and how they made claims in ways that opened up long-established cultural divisions – in Germany it was the Jews. It seems that the Germans bought into 'race as substitute for the nation' (Arendt 2009: 185). A second feature was how the construction of ideology was through the use of propaganda or 'traditionally accepted mysteries' (p351) and 'what convinces masses are not facts, and not even invented facts, but only the consistency of the system of which they are presumably part' (p351). So fabrications are crucial to the process of eliminating politics, and once in control there is no need for propaganda: 'systematic lying to the whole world can be safely

carried out only under the conditions of totalitarian rule, where the fictitious quality of everyday reality makes propaganda superfluous' (p413)

Total terror

Arendt (1970: 55) makes a distinction between violence and terror:

> Terror is not the same as violence; it is, rather, the form of government
> that comes into being when violence, having destroyed all power, does
> not abdicate but, on the contrary, remains in full control. It has often
> been noticed that the effectiveness of terror depends almost entirely on
> the degree of social atomization. Every kind of organized opposition
> must disappear before the full force of terror can be let loose.

Central to understanding this is how Arendt (2009) makes a distinction
between tyranny and totalitarianism: the former is about controlling opponents through fear and removal, the latter uses terror once opponents have
been eliminated; it is used to govern the innocent and obedient:

> Terror as we know it today strikes without any preliminary provoca-
> tion, its victims are innocent even from the point of view of the
> persecutor ... we are not concerned here with the ultimate conse-
> quence of the rule by terror – namely, that nobody, not even the execu-
> tors, can ever be free of fear; in our context we are dealing merely with
> the arbitrariness by which victims are chosen, and for this it is decisive
> that they are objectively innocent, that they are chosen regardless of
> what they may or may not have done.
>
> (Arendt 2009: 6)

Bowring (2011) argues that terror is not about managing change so that
people think and do differently, but to make other thinking seem illogical
and preposterous. Indeed, the death camps were not used as a warning
to others because 'these people were effectively dead before they
were murdered, for all traces and memories of their lives were made to
disappear' (Bowring 2011: 195).

Destruction of human bonds

Arendt (2009) identifies that total terror permeates into human relationships, even the most intimate, and removes the spaces for pluralism and
hence freedom: 'by using the permanent threat of betrayal to create an
atmosphere of paranoid distrust between family members, colleagues and

friends, totalitarian regimes sought to destroy all non-political bonds which might have formed a bulwark against the demands of the movement' (Bowring 2011: 19). The aim was to isolate in order to make the person feel powerful, but in reality the person is powerless because they are not authentically engaging with others. So totalitarianism is not a class, or party, or government, but is a mass movement 'of atomized, isolated individuals' (Arendt 2009: 323) with a 'demand for total, unrestricted, unconditional, and unalterable loyalty of the individual member' (p323). This happens because 'total loyalty is possible only when fidelity is emptied of all concrete content, from which changes of mind might naturally arise' (p324). This loyalty works in two ways: there is a combination of the active can do 'mob mentality' (p307) with the passivity of the masses who are responsive to capture or at least fail to overtly resist: 'potentially, they exist in every country and form the majority of those large numbers of neutral, politically indifferent people who never join a party and hardly ever go to the polls' (p311). Action and movement is what enables totalitarianism to sustain itself as people collaborate in various forms with activity:

> this impermanence no doubt has something to do with the proverbial fickleness of the masses and the fame that rests on them; more likely, it can be traced to the perpetual motion mania of totalitarian movements which can remain in power only so long as they keep moving and set everything around them in motion.
>
> (p306)

The adherents of totalitarian movements not only commit crimes against others, but also against themselves: 'he may even be willing to help in his own prosecution and frame his own death sentence if only his status as a member of the movement is not touched' (p307). It seems that while the state uses institutions to commit violence, it is the internal self that matters more because 'totalitarianism has discovered a means of dominating and terrorizing human beings from within' (p325).

Bureaucracy

Arendt (2009: 185) identified that 'bureaucracy . . . [became] . . . a substitute for government'. What had to happen was the communication of myths together with the necessary action to live those myths:

> the forms of totalitarian organization, as distinguished from their ideological content and propaganda slogans, are completely new. They

are designed to translate the propaganda lies of the movement, woven around a central fiction – the conspiracy of the Jews, or the Trotskyites, or 300 families, etc – into a functioning reality, to build up, even under non totalitarian circumstances, a society whose members act and react according to the rules of a fictitious world.

(p364)

Insiders know about the fabrications but they are 'complimented by totalitarian propaganda on that superior intelligence which supposedly distinguishes them from the nontotalitarian outside world' (p383). Indeed, 'so long as the movement exists, its peculiar form of organization makes sure that at least the elite formations can no longer conceive of a life outside the close knit band of men who, even if they are condemned, still feel superior to the rest of the uninitiated world' (p381). It is the link to the sympathisers and those who do not seemingly engage that requires the propaganda. Consequently, the Nazis constructed 'front organizations' (p364) before they took power as a means of distinguishing between party members and others, but also to enable communication:

the front organizations surround the movements' membership with a protective wall which separates them from the outside, normal world; at the same time, they form a bridge back into normalcy, without which the members in the prepower stage would feel too sharply the differences between their beliefs and those of normal people, between the lying fictitiousness of their own and the reality of the normal world.

(p366)

Once in power the front organisations are important in relation to the whole population who are 'now organized as sympathisers' (p413), and indeed the whole state becomes a front organisation, with:

sympathising bureaucrats whose function in domestic affairs is to spread confidence among the masses of merely co-ordinated citizens and whose foreign affairs consist in fooling the outside, nontotalitarian world. The Leader, in his dual capacity as chief of state and leader of the movement, again combined in his person the acme of militant ruthlessness and confidence inspiring normality.

(p413)

The leader within a totalitarian movement is not what the usual labels of 'despot', 'tyrant' and 'autocrat' suggest. This is not about a division of labour with a hierarchy, with the potential *coup d'état* combined with charisma and patriarchy, but is about 'total power' (p365) because 'totalitarian leaders are actually free to do whatever they please and can count on the loyalty of their entourage even if they choose to murder them' (p387). Succession is not based on rules or inheritance but the assumption to office where the leader and movement identify with each other, and so the person cannot be removed from office as it would threaten the 'infallibility' of the person and so the movement:

> it is not the truthfulness of the Leader's words but the infallibility of his actions which is the basis for the structure. Without it and in the heat of a discussion which presumes infallibility, the whole fictitious world of totalitarianism goes to pieces, overwhelmed at once by the factuality of the real world which only the movement steered in an infallibly right direction by the Leader was able to ward off.
>
> (p387)

Whereas most systems are a pyramid, a totalitarian regime is in Arendt's (2006a) terms an 'onion', where the leader is in a centre space, and all actions are from 'within, and not from without or above' (Arendt 2009: 99), and so:

> All the extraordinary manifold parts of the movement – the front organizations, the various professional societies, the party membership, the party bureaucracy, the elite formations, and police groups – are related in such a way that each forms the façade in one direction and the center in another, that is, plays the role of normal outside world for one layer and the role of radical extremism for another.
>
> (p99)

In summary, totalitarianism is about integrated isolationism: the person is isolated but feels they belong:

> totalitarian domination as a form of government is new in that it is not content with this isolation and destroys private life as well. It bases itself on loneliness, on the experience of not belonging to the world at all, which is among the most radical and desperate experiences of man.
>
> (p475)

There are certain consequences: first, as Schell (2006) argues, not only is the individual destroyed but also the means by which any resistance might develop, and so there is a need to examine the realities of people's lives as they experience totalitarianism; second, Canovan (1995) argues that Nazism was 'the breakdown of political and social structure, of authority and tradition and of the moral barriers against evil-doing', and she goes on to say that once this happened 'it was easy for the "gutter" to burst into politics, demonstrating how desperately fragile the dykes of civilisation were' (Canovan 1995: 158). Consequently, my task is to not only understand why totalitarianism happened in Germany and the Soviet Union at a particular time, but also to acknowledge that the conditions always remain, where crystallisation may not be recognised until it is too late. Indeed, as Arendt has argued (see Chapter 1), the social sciences did not have the methodologies to investigate such breaks in the human tradition.

Total leadership

Leaders doing leading and exercising leadership is everywhere in everyday life events and it crosses borders. It is in prime ministerial speeches (e.g. Blair 1998), it permeates popular professional texts (e.g. Stubbs 2003) and it is in claims about effective public practice (e.g. Giuliani with Kurson 2005). Claims are made for its vitality, necessity and direct relationship with successful outcomes. Much riches and acclaim await those who succeed, and those who transgress may face legal redress but also public approbation and isolation. I want to argue that the dominance of the TLP with a shift in emphasis in ELMA towards leaders, leading and leadership in public services means that totalitarian tendencies can be witnessed, and so like Fraser (2004: 254) I would like to ask: 'do today's dangers to humanity still arise from projects aimed at obliterating spontaneity and plurality? And do those dangers still stem from the same fateful conjunction of the nation-state's crisis with the proclivity for seeing like a state?'. ELMA is seemingly a benign and normal process, but the evidence shows that its design and delivery is about 'obliterating spontaneity and plurality', and this is rooted in the ongoing crisis in the nation state at a time of periodic globalised economic dislocation, where following the work of Scott (1998), reforms are designed and enacted through 'seeing like a state'.

Major interventions as a permanent revolution of modernising reforms are being made into complex organisational and communal exchange processes, which do not respect the values and practices of those who are rendered as the project to be reformed. Current models of preferred ELMA in public services are based on functional and normative categories, often labelled as 'standards', and through complying with this a person becomes 'stateless within a state' (Butler and Spivak 2010: 16). The call for transparency is, according to Strathern (2000), presented as innocent, but in reality teachers and children have been rendered stateless through the operation of targets, audit and measurement; they have been turned into disconnected and disembodied objects who produce the right type of data. The label New Public Management (NPM) has been used to chorale voices and suture together these complex and often contradictory modernisation strategies designed to secure efficiency, effectiveness and excellence (Hood 2007). Fragile success brings short-term higher pay, honours, potential celebrity status, with usually more work to do in the long term. The deficit of being identified as failing (as a learner, a teacher, a school) positions the person as superfluous, and this disconnects the person from political action. Instead, the child or teacher must be mentored, or work with a critical friend or consultant, and so politics is replaced by the confession of a crime (not doing homework, failing to reach targets, not producing the right type of lesson plan) and the adoption of an imaginary student or teacher identity. Butler and Spivak (2010) illuminate this type of situation by telling the story of how the US anthem was sung in Spanish in 2006, and how this was regarded by the Bush administration as un-American. Teachers and children are not allowed to speak about education in their language, they are mute in the face of 'improvement', 'effectiveness' and 'value-added data'. In summary, the potential enforced crystallisation of totalitarian conditions in the UK state through NPM (and the emerging New Public Leadership) restructuring and reculturing is shaping English schools and producing totalitarian tendencies. I intend to examine this through using Arendt's (2009) four categories.

Ideology

The fictitious world is that of the school as an efficient and effective business that transmits a particular moral code, where in England school life has been economised (Ball 2007), and in the US school life has been militarised (Saltman and Gabbard 2011). Through the implementation of various neoliberal projects over the past 30 years the school has had to adopt private sector language, cultures, roles and reward structures, and more recently private sector control of new forms of schools has been set up to residualise public schooling. In England the academies programme has enabled powerful interests to gain a stronger footing in public education, and the free schools are enabling private interests to dominate the education of children within a locality (Gunter 2011). Interrelated with this have been neoconservative projects regarding the traditionalism within the national curriculum combined with requirements for behaviour symbolised in the school uniform, the control of play and the use of punishments.

The fabrications on which this is based are located within the relationship between globalisation, as a modern-day form of imperialism, and totalitarianism. For example, Barber (2001) focuses on how equity can be delivered through directly linking education with economic competitiveness, and the exercise of school choice as a normal and accepted way of organising a public service. In Gewirtz's (2001) terms, all have to be cloned like the Blairs (and Thatchers, Majors, Camerons) with aspirations for economic and cultural success, based on a shared ontological and epistemological world of material gains through consumption by both elites and masses. Through what Bhabha (1994: 122) calls 'mimicry' the former regulate the latter, but while there are forms of 'resemblance' there are tensions between 'mockery' and 'menace' (p123). While elites and masses can both stake a credit card, it is the case that the masses get a glimpse of an elite life but cannot actually enter it, and as such the spectre of losing it all (debt, redundancy) is dangerous. In education this is being done by focusing on data-determined failure of pupils, teachers, headteachers and schools in the state system; promoting the independent private school as the best model for state schools to emulate; and the opening up of the curriculum, workforce composition and conditions of service and the student experience to private elite interests.

This is not a Marxist argument because as Arendt (1993) has argued this would have serious weaknesses, not least the claims that the economy is one step closer to a scientific dialectical 'once and for all' revolution. By examining the life and work of Rosa Luxemborg, Arendt (1993: 39) sheds light on dark times by showing that 'expropriation had to be repeated time and time again to keep the system in motion'. Consequently, the imaginings and fabrications in the neoliberal and neoconservative projects can be exposed by confronting and examining what is new about different types of market penetration into public services. So grant maintained status schools from 1988 through to free schools from 2010 are all examples of totalitarian tendencies under the guise of the freedom of new investment and choice opportunities. The momentum is maintained through the promotion of common sense beliefs, selected and commissioned evidence, and the urgency of change is driven by futuring. The enemy is identified as the public sector worker, who is economically unproductive because they do not work in 'for profit' services, are profligate with the taxpayers' money, and work in ways that are not responsive to consumer requirements. More extreme attacks are on the nature of democracy, and that schools should not be subject to community and democratic control. To paraphrase Arendt, it seems that the English have bought into economic productivity as a substitute for the welfare of the nation. However, the irony is that neoliberal and neoconservative projects need and feed off more and more centralised regulation, where successive secretaries of state have taken on more and new powers. Notably the direct funding of schools outside of local authorities based on individual agreements has led Wilby (2012: unpaged) to comment that England is in the midst of 'the creation of a fully centralised school system in which the secretary of state for education has the powers of an elected dictator'. The construction and transmission of ELMA is such that the knowledge base and the skills required to enact officially designed good practice is about fitting in with this top-down model. While the rhetoric is one of agency and entrepreneurialism, in reality the job of the headteacher is to locally deliver externally determined requirements. Those who claim agency are in effect reworking the preferred model of leadership rather than doing anything new or innovative (Gunter 2012a).

Total terror

The identification of tyranny and the experience of terror as a destructive process within education is within our scholarship (e.g. Ball 2003), and recently Coffield and Williamson (2012) have articulated the situation:

> There are powerful forces at work in the modern world telling people how they should imagine their future lives. The worst excesses of the twentieth century were perpetrated by men and women who knew what they wanted the future to be and imposed their will on their societies. The madmen have not gone away. We have a new lot. As before, too many people are trapped in circumstances that leave them unable to challenge the ideas of those seeking the power to define their future.
>
> (Coffield and Williamson 2012: 14)

Certainly tyranny exists in the removal of opponents: first, the identification of failing heads and teachers through data-driven judgements based on arbitrary determined 'benchmarked' boundaries, such as the calculation of how many per cent of children have passed five GCSE examinations between the grades of A* through to C, and how many have English and maths, and then how many have English, maths, a science, a foreign language and a humanity. Second, the removal of professional credentials, creativity and judgement through managerialist audits, workforce remodelling and the linkage with pay and contract renewal has turned teaching and learning into a delivery process (known as teaching to the test) which does not need professional training and accreditation, and so is open to the market; and, third, the requirement for simultaneously enthusiastic and compliant dispositions in professional practice has led to the marginalisation of alternative ideas and evidence, where the proclivity for debate, and the people who promote this, have been rendered enemies.

Disposability of teachers is evident (see Butt and Gunter 2007, Gunter and Hall 2013, Gunter 2011), where, for example, the HMCI Sir Michael Wilshaw recently declared that 5,000 headteachers are not up to standard because they use excuses for poor performance rather than exercise leadership to deliver higher standards: 'we are not going to improve the quality of teaching unless there is a) strong leadership and b) really strong performance management of staff' (Clark 2012: unpaged). The impact of this on the workforce is that, 'I could be next', particularly when schools are being converted into academies where terms and conditions of service are changed and free schools are being set up without trained teachers. In Arendt's (2009) terms public sector workers and teachers have become 'social pariahs' and this is a political issue because 'they make no effort to transform the political status or the political meanings that attach to their social position. In short, they embrace their abject position without mounting a significant political challenge to the grounds of their exclusion' (p25). Consequently, there is the potential for a shift from tyranny, or the removal of opponents, to totalitarianism where those who supported the exiting of poor teachers and heads now experience the disappearance of themselves (see Gunter 2005, Yarker 2005).

Destruction of human bonds

The officially endorsed approach to ELMA in England is destructive of human relationships, and so the informal bonds that link people through shared routes into the job and professional experiences are eradicated. The school as a business, where everyone is involved in delivering and demonstrating the totality of performance, means that relationships are based on transactions and calculated exchanges known as 'collaboration' rather than trusted cooperation (Gunter and Hall 2012, Sennett 2012). The official model of effective and efficient functional leadership is 'transformational', where the heroic and charismatic headteacher is expected to motivate and inspire, speak to individual needs and aspirations, influence the thinking and imagination of subordinates and communicate in ways that build an emotional commitment to a vision (Gunter 2001a). This preferred leadership model has been redesigned and reworked (e.g. Leithwood *et al.* 2006) but the core remains intact: the job of the head is to control staff, pupils and parents in such a way that national reforms are effectively and efficiently delivered locally. This has been enabled through training and professional development as 'make-overs' where the individual professional has been invited into a status-improving process where they learn to take on private sector purposes, rationales and narratives (Gunter and Thomson 2009). They have been given the rules that enable them to know and present themselves as knowledgeable about all aspects of ELMA, and so they seek loyalty and a 'can do' approach rather than debate and analyse. Local activity is in reality about tactical implementation as strategy is decided elsewhere, and so an effective leader ensures that what needs to be done is done. So pluralism and the debates that have gone on historically within and about professional practice are denied, and this can be illustrated by comparing headteacher accounts of their role from the 1970s with the current day (see Gunter and Thomson 2010). Headteachers do demonstrate a proclivity to learn and to think about the role (see Ribbins 1997) but Stubbs' (2003) account is about getting rid of teachers who won't work in the way that she requires them to. The intensity of action and doing things is central to current headteacher accounts of turning around failing schools (see also Clark 1998), where compliance is perhaps the most damaging of all common sense things to do.

Bureaucracy

The myths surrounding ELMA have been promoted in government texts and supported by commissioned projects. Language is central to the fabrications and lies across all educational institutions; it has been described in higher education by Inglis (2011) as the 'monstrosity of managerial vocabulary':

> One of the most painful injuries inflicted on any sensitive and intelligent person on becoming head of department is the lowering language that has then to fill your mouth, with the dreadful polysyllabic phrases that, once swallowed, prove immediately emetic. All that 'prioritising', 'operational implications', 'outcome indicators', 'impact beneficiaries', 'incremental significance', and 'levels of robustness' . . .
>
> (Inglis 2011: 38)

This adoption of a new vocabulary is linked to status. For example, the green paper *Teachers: meeting the challenge of change* (DfEE 1998) is stylish in design, promotes performance and audit as central to the modern professional, but speaks in ways that contain lies (e.g. about teacher appraisal, see Gunter 2001b) and unsubstantiated assertions about the centrality of headteachers as leaders. A mythology about ELMA that spoke to the leader-centric culture in England, and the traditional acceptance of a leading professional at the top of the pyramid, was not challenged, and government investment in leadership research was widely welcomed. While there were minor skirmishes regarding working conditions and pay, the myth of the teacher as failing children and parents was not rebuffed, and it seems this created income generation opportunities through professional development programmes. The sense of being part of a fast-moving and modernising movement created energy for making a difference. But the language and culture made it increasingly difficult to speak out, because the generation of alternative agendas was seen as disloyal and dangerous: a person who did speak out could very easily be characterised as not interested in children, learning, improvement and effectiveness. The optimism and modernism of 'front organisations' such as the National College also made it difficult, particularly as major investment was being made in the profession and into the necessary research that was demanded by leadership scholars.

The neoliberal and neoconservative myths combined with the promotion of private sector ELMA captured the profession, and required collaborators and popularisers who worked in and with the National College in ways that interconnected with the wider profession and public as sympathisers. The role of the National College is to deliver policy and so ensure that educational professionals are trained to accept and implement, and if they have a problem to handle it locally without disrupting roll out and data collection. So a networked TLP informed group of trusted professionals, researchers and international gurus was brought in to develop this, where dissent was not a possibility as these assumed politically neutral knowledge workers supported the changes and handled localised concerns, and if they were uncomfortable they waited until the situation was more congenial and they could offer new products. It was cold outside the 'tent' and those who failed were dealt with ruthlessly (see Beckett 2007, Gunter 2012a). Consequently the approach to ELMA was based on narrow forms of knowledge and knowing, and a few knowers who mainly did not address the growing critique of what was going on. Myths and mythologising was such that the National College did not need to answer for the limited knowledge base that its programmes and research was based on, because alternative work and knowledge workers did not exist in the imagined world of the effective and improving school, and if they sought recognition it was easy to discount them as irrelevant and destructive.

It is very easy to characterise the New Labour TLP colonisation of school leadership as rational and stable, but while the National College did dominate it is the case that other rival centres developed through the Specialist Schools and Academies Trust, and the academies programme led to chains of academies where owners sought to design and establish their own corporate leadership brand. So the front organisations were replicated in ways that show a 'deliberate shapelessness' (Bowring 2011: 198), with funding being used to invest in contradictory and often inefficient ways. Claims for authority and direction of professional ELMA training thus did get confused, but the overall message (or operating like the 'will of the fuhrer') is that ELMA matters and so should be accepted and practised.

This analysis of the conditions of totalitarianism within the TLP promotion and delivery of ELMA as a policy reform strategy suggests that education has been and continues to be in dark times. However, in following Arendt (1993) I do want to make the case that there is scholarly research that can and does make a difference:

> that even in the darkest of times we have the right to expect some illumination, and that such illumination may well come less from theories and concepts than from the uncertain, flickering, and often weak light that some men and women, in their lives and their works, will kindle under almost all circumstances and shed over the time span that was given them on earth . . . Eyes so used to darkness as ours will hardly be able to tell whether their light was the light of a candle or that of a blazing sun.
>
> (Arendt 1993: ix–x)

The first point to make is that 'totalitarian elements do not necessarily lead to totalitarianism' (Young-Bruehl 1982: xxiii), and so while McCarthyism in the US generated analysis of the existence of totalitarian conditions it did not develop into full-blown totalitarianism. What seems to matter is how the conditions 'crystallize' into totalitarianism (Jalušič 2007: 149), particularly through the way inclusion and exclusion of identified types or communities operates, and so Young-Bruehl (1982: xxiii–xxiv) argues that this is because there was no mass support or 'clear ideology' that unites disparate groups. Indeed, as Hood and Peters (2004) have argued, 'the middle aging' (p267) of NPM shows that the normative claims of reformers have not been borne out in practice, where unintended consequences and paradoxes have resulted from 'the casual adoption of poorly grounded models, the disregard of historical evidence, and a selective approach to evidence and indeed active resistance to learning in any meaningful sense' (p278). It seems that for all the investment in the emerging NPL it could be that underneath the rhetoric and lies there remain some truths and those who are prepared to think and speak them. Consequently Fraser (2004) argues in favour of 'modified adjectival forms as "proto-totalitarian" and "quasi-totalitarian" ' (p260), and so what is necessary is recognition of political action that is taking place regarding demythologising and making public alternative ways of doing research.

Canovan (1995) argues that Arendt's (2009) analysis shows that 'common sense morality' and 'religion' and 'philosophy' could not prevent totalitarianism (Canovan 1995: 161–162) and what matters is the importance of thinking and acting politically, because Arendt's:

> experience of Nazism, and of the weakness of alternative barriers against political evil, led her to the conclusion that our best safeguard is the deliberate building of republics to guarantee equal rights, and the defence of those republics by citizens who understand what they are defending.
>
> (Canovan 1995: 163)

So new and spontaneous beginnings are possible:

> The turning point that decides whether a one-party system will remain a dictatorship or develop into a form of totalitarian rule always comes when every last trace of active or passive opposition in the country has been drowned in blood and terror. Genuinely totalitarian terror, however, sets in only when the regime has no more enemies who can be arrested and tortured to death and when even the different classes of suspects are eliminated and can no longer be taken into 'protective custody'.
>
> (Arendt 1994: 298–299)

The plurality within the nation state is evident through the ongoing challenges to the 'elective dictatorship' (Hailsham 1976) of the unitary state and executive power, not least through various 'Occupy' campaigns (see: http://occupywallst.org), and the challenge to the inequalities in wealth through 'tent cities' springing up in major cities around the world. The plurality within the profession and wider communities remains in a number of ways, where independent research shows: first, there is evidence that headteachers have sought to position themselves differently to preferred leadership models (Gunter and Forrester 2009); second, students and parents are not automatically accepting major reforms such as academies (Hatcher and Jones 2006), and there are alternative ways of thinking about public services than through markets and consumer choice (Hatcher 2012); third, knowledge production outside of official government regimes and networks is robust and making a difference to scholarship and professional practice (Gunter 2012a, Wrigley *et al.* 2012a); and, fourth, research evidence that shows how postgraduate study (taught masters and research doctorates) is attractive to the profession because it enables social justice goals to be investigated and realised (Taysum and Gunter 2008).

Canovan (1995) enables the problematics of Arendt's thinking on 'radical evil' (p157) to be examined through how 'the political evil she confronted wore two faces, one right-wing and one left, each of them raising questions of greater complexity' (p157). The adoption of neoliberal and neoconservative projects by both left- and right-wing governments in England is illustrative of these 'two faces', but while it seems there are totalitarian conditions and trends, the continued existence of research 'enemies' acts as a bulwark. This requires more investigation, and in the next two chapters I focus on professional practice in more depth.

4 Using Arendt to think about ELMA

The *vita activa*

Introduction

This chapter will confront the policies of successive governments who bought into the TLP and so have framed and promoted ELMA as both organisational (school) and systemic (market) performance leadership. Drawing on Arendt's (1958) text *The Human Condition*, the chapter will use data to examine the nature of labour, work and action, and it will consider the rhetorical construction of leadership as action and juxtapose it with the realities of labour and work. In doing so the chapter reconfirms Arendt's arguments that action and politics are important, and so I will use this to generate questions about the composition of the school workforce, the nature of professional practice and the interplay between agency and structure in the experience of professional identity construction. In doing so I am well aware that *The Human Condition*, like other texts, is contentious because it is 'regarded by some as a work of genius and by others as beneath refutation' (Canovan 1998: xv). The left are troubled by Arendt's arguments on the social because they could be interpreted as being anti-social but her analysis of action has given inspiration to civil rights activists (Canovan 1998).

Labour

Let me begin with two stories.

Story 1 is from Mary, headteacher of Ash Primary School, who was interviewed as part of the Knowledge Production in Educational Leadership (KPEL) Project (Gunter 2012a):

> I think first of all we have got to say that education, education, education was fantastic and music to our ears and that the government has put education on the map and they have actually funded it extremely

well and are continuing to do so. So I am delighted in that respect. And yes the initiatives have come in fast and furious. Many of them, I think, have been very good and they have certainly made us sharpen school improvement, they have made us look at policy and practice, and that's something as a school needs to be ever evolving anyway to meet the needs to the children. I think what can happen and probably what many, many people feel is that they are overburdened with this and that initiative, but I think if you can sift and if you can take the good that is really going to support the needs of your children then it's very good. If there is something that you feel is not going to have a great impact, perhaps you may pay lip service, or you may feel that it isn't going to have an impact on our school, and I think that's what it's all about. Nobody wants anybody to completely change their school, but the new initiatives are there for you to pick out what good parts would serve the needs of your children. And I think you know it's having perhaps the experience and the skills to be able to do that. Otherwise, yes you can become overburdened and you know you have your in-tray and you have your out-tray, you know what goes in your in-tray that is very important that you need to take action, and that which is out.

(Gunter 2008: unpaged)

Story 2 is from Yarker (2005), where he recounts what happened when his daughter brought home a letter from school regarding the remodelling of the school workforce, with particular attention given to higher level teaching assistants taking on a teaching role:

I admired how the letter told it straight: 'to *teach* to their skills and experience'. But support-staff support: only teachers teach. I wrote back raising my concerns. I was replied to. An afternoon per week of planning, preparation and assessment time (PPA) had enabled teachers to achieve real progress in dealing with their workload. Various options were being tested 'trying to ensure that the pupils continue to receive education from qualified teachers wherever possible . . . However, regardless of my own personal views, I have been charged as Acting Headteacher with ensuring that a system of PPA is imple-mented for September 2005, it being a legal requirement.' Reading this, I was struck less by the submission to the force of the law than by the self-censorship. At no point in her letter had the Acting Headteacher in fact divulged her personal views. I still do not know what she thinks about Workforce Remodelling. But I think her silence is telling.

(Yarker 2005: 170)

Both of these stories can generate positive responses: Story 1 is an account of how school leadership is about mediating the external demands for modernisation with knowledge and understanding of the school combined with the art of the possible; Story 2 shows how regulation of working conditions and the composition of the workforce can enable teachers to have an appropriate workload. Both of these stories illuminate what Arendt (1958) called 'labour':

> Labour is the activity which corresponds to the biological process of the human body, whose spontaneous growth, metabolism, and eventual decay are bound to the vital necessities produced and fed into the life process by labor. The human condition of labor is life itself.
>
> (Arendt 1958: 7)

Essentially, both stories are about the basic need to survive. Ash Primary School is about reading the initiatives and pragmatically responding, and Yarker's story of the primary school is about compliance with a national agreement. Consequently, leadership in both stories is about production and consumption of what is necessary to endure, it is cyclical and repetitious with no creativity or longevity beyond the immediate gratification of having done the job and consumed the product. So in designing and implementing change projects there is no claim for status based on creativity in the curriculum or pedagogic innovation; instead claims are about having done what was necessary to keep a job. It is about '*animal laborans*' (Arendt 1958: 136) where activity is located in 'worldlessness'. The delivery approach is about producing the right type of data: at Ash Primary School the 'sifting' process can only happen if the school is meeting national standards, and Yarker's account of the acting primary headteacher shows that there is no attempt to look for spaces for discretion. At both schools the emphasis is on getting things right: at Ash Primary the management of the 'in' and 'out' trays is what matters; in Yarker's account it is about the deployment of non-teachers to teach children. Interestingly Yarker (2005) asks questions that generate interrelationships with totalitarian conditions: 'how far is it proper for a teacher to stay silent, or to be silenced and to disregard their personal views, in the implementation of education policy?' (p170). It seems that educational purposes are decided elsewhere and the headteacher as labourer delivers approved of outcomes and manages the situation locally.

Interestingly, Arendt (1958) argues that labour does not have high status, and even though claims for recognition are within the two stories, there is evidence of low status: project implementation and statistical data are fleeting because satisfaction, like food as a survival need, is temporary. Arendt (1958) goes on to argue that much of the human condition has been turned into labour, and so while the two schools might gain approval for what they are doing it is because it is labour. In other words, both schools may think they are involved in strategy and yet in reality what they are doing is tactical and technical implementation; both schools may think they are close to policymakers because they are involved in the modernisation of the system, but in reality they are giving professional legitimacy to decisions made by people who put marketisation and for-profit developments before children as learners; both schools may think they are engaged in school improvement and may claim that what they are doing is on behalf of children, but in reality they are displacing educational opportunities with a testing and accountability regime. So labour is more than the intensification of activity, it is about the type of practices that are being undertaken, and while professionals are busy doing this then they do not connect it to wider shifts in the dismantling of education as a public service.

Work

Here are two more stories.

Story 3: I was part of an evaluation team for a government project (Thomas *et al.* 2004, Butt and Gunter 2007), and this is an illustrative account, based on the data and written by myself, of how a school was handling pressures to develop a more flexible workforce:

> Poplar High School was part of a government funded evaluation of a major intervention into the composition and professional practice of the workforce. In 2002 the then New Labour Government launched the *Transforming the School Workforce Pathfinder Project* where 32 schools experimented with the increase in non-teaching staff as a proportion of the workforce (e.g. teaching assistants, clerical support, student services), and the use of ICT to support administrative systems (e.g. student registration) and support for learning (e.g. access to lesson plans and learning resources). In one school they removed the books from the library and replaced them with over one hundred computers staffed by one teaching assistant who could support the children and two security staff who were employed to prevent damage to the equipment. The idea was based on the need to trial online learning and reducing staff time spent on covering lessons due to staff absence. So if a member of staff was absent a class could be sent to

this learning centre and they could complete work through online packages.

Story 4: Linda, headteacher of Elm High School, was interviewed as part of the Knowledge Production in Educational Leadership (KPEL) Project (Gunter 2012a):

> This is an inner city school, this is a school in challenging circum-
> stances. There was 8% A*–C when I came here, school was split
> between two sites, 77% attendance, falling rolls, deficit budget, low
> aspirations in the community and indeed in the school, three failing
> departments. And kids and staff travelled up and down the road a mile
> and a half a day on buses and in cars. Now we have a 41% 5 A*–C,
> new buildings, further new building next year. Special Performing
> Arts College, Extended Pilot School for [city name]. Full in every year
> group with waiting lists. And of the 91 staff I have appointed 69 of
> them. So they are young, bright eyed, bushy tailed staff and we're
> also a training school. So a lot of people who have joined up to the
> vision and focus of the school. And so I think that has an effect on
> young people . . . when I first came to the school only 25% accessed
> post 16, now 72% are. We are getting kids into universities now . . .
> so only four of our parents in a survey which we did last year have
> been to university and only two of those straight from school, the
> others had done it by the Open University. And we have had two kids
> in recent years getting into Oxbridge. So that really you know makes
> me feel good.
>
> (Gunter 2008: unpaged)

Both of these stories can generate positive responses: Story 3 shows how a school is effectively and efficiently managing staff resources, where instead of losing non-contact time due to staff absence a teacher can get on with their preparation and marking, and children can have access to learning resources; and Story 4 is an account of success, the school has been turned around with important gains in student outcomes being reported.

There are links here with Arendt's (1958) arguments about labour, as there is a survival and survivor narrative involved. Poplar High School had been given funds as part of a pilot project to experiment with new ways of managing the school workforce that could be scaled up across the system, and so prevent teachers from leaving the profession. Elm High School was in danger of failing and so needed to undertake activity that would change the data and so demonstrate that education is better because the test scores have improved. So ELMA is based on acclaim for having done things in externally approved of ways, where recognition and approval are central to the ongoing and never satiated process of surviving.

However, something more can be identified in the stories, and this is what Arendt (1958) refers to as work. Work generates products that have some durability and the potential to outlive the creator:

> Work is the activity which corresponds to the unnaturalness of human existence, which is not imbedded in, and whose morality is not compensated by, the species' ever-recurring life cycle. Work provides an 'artificial' world of things, distinctly different from all natural surroundings. Within its borders each individual life is housed, while this world itself is meant to outlast and transcend them all. The human condition of work is worldliness.
>
> (Arendt 1958: 7)

It is about '*homo faber* who makes and literally "works upon"' which 'fabricates the sheer unending variety of things whose sum total constitutes the human artifice' (Arendt 1958: 136). As Bowring (2011) states:

> Arendt appears to include both material objects like buildings, tools and works of art, and the less tangible but not necessarily less durable forms of cultural, legal and political institutions, including the 'web' of human relationships and narratives, and shapes the way actors are understood, responded to and remembered.
>
> (Bowring 2011: 18)

There is evidence of this at both schools: at Poplar the design and implementation of a project that has set up a learning centre is an example of work, and at Elm clear changes have taken place in regard to the curriculum, staffing (e.g. job descriptions, structures as well as people) and new buildings are examples of work. In addition to this both schools have aimed to establish different working relationships with staff and students, with the building of a commitment to the headteacher's vision. Linda explains this through her acceptance of, and recognition for, being a transformational leader and doing transformation:

> I was invited four years ago to a meeting in London by the DfES. I hadn't a clue why I was, and there were about 200 of us there nationally. And that was because we had been identified as being transformational leaders. And it had come through a whole variety of OfSTED reports, knowledge from the DfES of you, LEA recommendations and

so on. And it was interesting and there were two of us there from [city name], and I am now part of that network which I find to be very good . . . I suppose I am a charismatic leader.

(Gunter 2008: unpaged)

While Linda's narrative goes on to show that she recognises that a person does not have to be charismatic to be a transformational leader, she does emphasise the importance of this for herself in how power is exercised. Notably she shows how her agency within a network of headteachers is supported and enabled in ways that have durability, not least through her own learning, and how she builds on this over time and joins it up across a range of projects and innovations. In doing this she not only structures her own location in the world but also that of others who learn from her professional practice.

So there is evidence of work through the relationship between transformation and products and labour. However, the opportunity always exists that work becomes labour, particularly since agreements on what constitutes the purposes of education and the strategies developed to deliver on this are made outside of schools. What is missing from the four stories presented so far is a sense of natality or doing something new through taking action. It is to this that I now turn.

Action

While the four stories may lay claim to illuminating something new and transformational, in reality much of what is taking place is more of the same but usually rebranded, and is based on existing power structures that limit participation in decisions to powerful elites. All four stories illuminate modernisation projects that are about deprofessionalising teachers through removing professional judgement and discretion and replacing it with technical data generation and analysis, and high stakes accountability through contract renewal/termination. The powerful people in education are business sponsors who make reforms work, government civil servants who award and manage projects, and ministers who demand data to prove that policies are working. While professionals are working hard in schools to make changes, and like Mary and Linda can claim to make decisions and seek spaces for discretion, in reality this is about tactics and pragmatism. The workforce have learned to labour, and in some cases to do hard labour, and some have been able to carve out a way of handling this that is productive for them and has as sense of durability about it.

The structuring of professional practice as mainly labour with some features of work has impacted on children. They have become the objects of the labour and work processes, and while claims are made that reforms are done in the interests of children, there are two issues that Arendt would identify in the analysis so far: first, that like 'Little Rock' children are being required to resolve adult problems: using online packages to demonstrate that learning can still take place under the supervision of non-qualified teachers; and providing data to demonstrate school improvement. Second, that like her analysis in 'Crisis in education' adults are not taking responsibility for enabling children to understand the world, and instead are providing children with a narrow technical approach that education is about economic productivity. Taking responsibility in these cases shows that at Elm School, and the school described by Yarker, teachers are on board with a vision that they have not created; at Poplar teachers are in the staffroom doing marking and preparation while children use computers under surveillance by a security team; and at Ash School teachers face the consequences of decisions about the in-tray and out-tray. Arendt (1958) is helpful in thinking differently about labour and work as the dominant professional practice by focusing on the importance of action. Here I present two more stories that illuminate.

Story 5 is from Barry, the headteacher of Oak High School, who was interviewed as part of the KPEL project (Gunter 2012a):

> I suppose in a sense it's about wanting to make a difference I guess, it's about fundamentally wanting to work to increase the capacity of young people to take responsibility and ownership of their own world, but not in an atomised sense but in a sense of working on behalf of others to create a better world. So we have that idealistic view of why we're there and what we're trying to do so it is two-fold really. One, it's about a commitment to build a society and then it's about a commitment to try to find for the young people that you work with something about the talents and treasures that they have and finding ways of working with them so those talents become really polished and enable them to do what they want to do. But I suppose the third element . . . is that for every child to make sure that the squalor of the past isn't repeated because people are constantly abused . . . And I think fear has a lot to do with ignorance and a lot to do with people in the sense of living in the atomised world rather than in an effective world. So the third part of a commitment to being a head I think is about making sure that every single individual is not in a position to be abused, but is in a position to be able to rationalise and make sense of their own world on behalf of themselves and for others.
>
> (Gunter 2008: unpaged)

Story 6 is from Kingswood High School where I have worked with Thomson (Gunter and Thomson 2006, see also Hollins *et al.* 2006) on a students as researchers project, and more recently with McGinity (McGinity and Gunter 2012) on the school learning policy project. Based on the experience of this research I have written this illustrative account:

> Kingswood High School is an officially successful comprehensive school in England, and has spent the past decade working on developing a research culture and researcher dispositions among staff and students. The approach taken by the headteacher has been to establish broad agreement with staff, students and parents regarding educational and school purposes, and has built on this to develop school policies towards teaching and learning, and the role of children in local policymaking. This has not been a smooth and linear process within school, particularly since professional created changes are generally not given recognition by official visits from inspectors. However, the school has been able to sustain an approach to primary research, and there are two examples of this: first, the 'students as researchers project' enabled a team of students to decide on a substantial and important topic for research, and they then designed, delivered and communicated the findings in ways that influenced policy, and a strategy to continue to involve students in research and policy. Second, the 'learning policy project' is based on the school's recognition that while they are developing an official learning culture that is widely supported, there are issues about how social class operates to include/exclude children in ways that impact on relationships and achievement. Both projects are school initiated, and they are based on a partnership between the school and higher education.

Both of these stories illuminate issues of labour and work: both schools are part of the national standards agenda and must be seen to generate data that is calculated in ways that result in approved of education, and both schools engage in activity that is more than survival through the artefacts produced (e.g. buildings, learning outputs from essays through to sculpture) and networked relationships within and external to the schools. However, there is something more in these narratives that needs attention, and Arendt (1958) is helpful in developing understandings of this through her distinctive definition of action.

Action lifts humans from the consumption utility of labour and the solitary crafting of work. In both stories there is a sense of doing things that are worthwhile and enduring, and located in plurality as: 'the condition of human action because we are all the same, that is, human, in such a way that nobody is ever the same as anyone else who ever lived, lives, or will live' (Arendt 1958: 8). In both stories children are conceptualised as people who are different and so engagement with them must begin on this basis: 'action, the only activity that goes on directly between men without the intermediary of things or matter, corresponds to the human condition of plurality, to the fact that men, not Man, live on the earth and inhabit the world' (Arendt 1958: 7).

Action is based on natality or the endless capacity to do something new and spontaneous:

> The miracle that saves the world, the realm of public affairs, from its normal, 'natural' ruin is ultimately the fact of natality, in which the faculty of action is ontologically rooted. It is, in other words, the birth of new men and the new beginning, the action they are capable of by virtue of being born.
>
> (Arendt 1958: 247)

There is a sense of active agency in Stories 5 and 6, where thinking about issues, recognising the complexity of the world in which they and the school are located, and focusing on what matters to them is normal. Whereas in Stories 1-4 there is a sense that agency is fabricated, either nationally through training, networking and contractual delivery arrangements or locally through getting things done and being seen to get things done through the narration of metrics. What seems to have happened is that in western style democracies, there is an acceptance that the power to determine what is to be done lies away from the citizen and is located in elite people and institutions, and so 'accepting the principle of sovereignty as a replacement for that of free action can in Arendt's view only result in either the arbitrary domination of a people or else their stoical withdrawal from the sphere of public life' (Bowring 2011: 37).

Action is what happens with and between people, and power is the property of a group (Arendt 1970). Humans are both conditioned and do conditioning through action: 'human existence is conditioned existence' (Arendt 1958: 9) but 'the conditions of human existence – life itself, natality and mortality, worldliness, plurality, and the earth – can never "explain" what we are or answer the question of who we are for the simple reason that they never condition us absolutely' (p11). So there always remains the potential for spontaneity: 'The presumption that the results of action can be known in advance, like the results of natural and productive processes, so that the main problem of politics becomes finding the means to achieve those results is what Arendt . . . rejects' (Kohn 2006: ix). Action is about thinking, talking, doing things. Whereas filling in a form for an inspector, writing a mission statement, or answering a parent who claims that their child will get a better education elsewhere, are all forms of labour with some potential for work, but taking action is something different:

> Action, as distinguished from fabrication, is never possible in isolation; to be isolated is to be deprived of the capacity to act. Action and speech need the surrounding presence of others no less than fabrication needs the surrounding presence of nature for its material, and of a world in which to place the finished product. Fabrication is surrounded by and in constant contact with the world: action and speech are surrounded by and in constant contact with the web of the acts and words of other men.
>
> (Arendt 1958: 188)

So the whole panoply of performance management of adults and children with targets and metrics is an isolating process: it is the individual who is responsible and accountable. Consequently, there are no opportunities for action. What makes Stories 5 and 6 distinctive is that there are clear attempts to take action: there is thinking about and with others regarding the purposes of education and how professional practices can be designed to work for these, and there are actions regarding curriculum design that frame learning and the recognition of that learning as something other than measurement. Morality and values are important, and what distinguishes these stories from the others is the emphasis on what Wright (2003) calls 'first order values' that focus on purposes within a socially unjust world. What Stories 1–4 seem to claim are 'second order values' of teams, collaboration and improvement (Wright 2003), in ways that are seductive and legitimising for those who seek to substitute such labour and work for action.

Plurality for the self as thinker and with others through dialogue is not borne out of necessity like labour but is valued for what it is. Arendt (1958) had become concerned that politics had become about rulership and government, but for her politics is about the space between humans that allows both distinction and similarity, and hence exchange. As Bowring (2011) argues, it is about 'worldliness' where through action a person takes care of the world and this 'resides neither in the maker nor in the thing made, but in the "space of appearances" where tastes are communicated and decisions about the common world are shared' (Bowring 2011: 25–26). Objectivity of the world is created through a range of positions, perceptions and possibilities, and so there is a distinction of the public world from the private. Understanding this can be helped through Arendt's

(1958) metaphor of sitting at the table, where people are both together and separate:

> To live together in the world means essentially that a world of things is between those who have it in common, as a table is located between those who sit around it; the world, like every in-between, relates and separates men at the same time.
>
> (Arendt 1958: 52)

This in-between world where action takes place is based on promises and forgiveness: stability is created through the making of promises and forgiveness happens when people transgress. Arendt (1958) argues that forgiveness is a form of freedom, because it is based on the reversal of what is said and done; this is integral to political activity. What dominates Stories 1–4 is a sense of contractual technical promising to deliver to a pre-designed standard (or signing on the bottom line) which denies the possibility for forgiveness: someone who does not deliver is dispensed with. There is no natality with the possibility to start something new, because modernisation captures the new and is premised on predictable certainty and delivery, and the emphasis on this has meant that action has been displaced by work and labour.

People may actually sit at a table to discuss targets and data, but action is reduced through the performativity within NPM. People are so squeezed together that thinking and talking and acting cannot take place, and there is a real danger of talking about the self in public as a substitute for the public world. Stories 1–4 illuminate how in a modern world people are invited to suppress their ideas and contribution in favour of teamwork and vision and mission, and so conformism is what dominates. The school as a public space is closed down. As I have already argued in Chapter 3, this is a condition of totalitarianism, where Stories 1–4 present noise and can do actions, but illuminate the lack of action. While concerns might be raised about the volume and speed of reforms, there are no substantive challenges to labour and work, and no alternatives:

> Action was soon and still is almost exclusively understood in terms of making and fabricating, only that making, because of its worldliness and inherent indifference to life was now regarded as but another form of labouring, a more complicated but not a more mysterious function of the life process.
>
> (Arendt 1958: 322)

Stories 5 and 6 provide a sense of publicness – that education is for the public and done with and on behalf of the public, and that larger issues of social justice matter. Here adults are taking responsibility for enabling children to understand the world as unjust and how the world might be different, and while children participate in decisions and policymaking they do so on the basis of pedagogic relationships.

Vita activa

Labour, work and action are linked to both birth and death, but action is what makes inhabiting the earth matter:

> Labor assures not only individual survival, but the life of the species. Work and its product, the human artifact, bestow a measure of permanence and durability upon the futility of mortal life and the fleeting character of human time. Action, in so far as it engages in founding and preserving political bodies, creates the condition for remembrance, that is, for history.
>
> (Arendt 1958: 8–9)

So as Bowring (2011: 22) states: 'work remedies the worldlessness of labour, and action remedies the meaninglessness of work', and Kohn (2006: xiv) argues that the three are hierarchial: 'in the sense that the specific ways human beings labor to sustain their lives are intelligible only in relation to the ways they work, just as the specific ways they work – building houses and constructing cities – are intelligible only in relation to the ways they act'. But action does not grow out of labour and work, it is based on humans who through their birthright have freedom through action:

> actions interrupt ongoing processes of labor and work and initiate new processes, which in turn are subject to interruption by further actions. The plurality of beings capable of action is the sole condition from which the realm of politics arises, not from a contract made in a primordial state of nature to establish some measure of human freedom, but from the election of those who are already free to live together with some measure of stability.
>
> (Kohn 2006: xiv)

So central to Arendt's analysis of the world is the importance of action located in politics as the space to share and exchange views, to debate and deliberate. However, action within ELMA continues to be threatened through the construction and implementation of neoliberal and neoconservative TLP modernisation projects by successive governments, and embedded within such projects is the elevation of labour and work. Social science research has identified a number of features of this, where, for example, the nature and vitality of the public domain is recognised as under severe threat (Marquand 2004, Sennett 2002) from audit (Power 1999) and 'the government of risk' (Hood *et al.* 2004). Illuminative examples show the extent that a person's character is experiencing 'corrosion' in the workplace (Sennett 1999) and in social relations particular groups are scapegoated in the name of a respect agenda (Squires 2008).

Arendt's take on this was to raise questions about the rise of the social realm and the damage this has done to the public realm. For Arendt, freedom is located not in the claims for social equity, but in political processes: 'equality, therefore, far from being connected with justice, as in modern times, was the very essence of freedom: to be free meant to be free from the inequality present in rulership and to move in a sphere where neither rule nor being ruled existed' (Arendt 1958: 33). What Arendt identifies is the growth of functions that generate control and are dependent on predictability, and the blurring of the private and public: 'the rise of the social coincided historically with the transformation of the private care for private property into a public concern' (Arendt 1958: 68). Consequently, government was constituted as being about the protection of wealth, and so private possessions rather than sharing of ideas is what the public realm has become:

> The rather uncomfortable truth of the matter is that the triumph the modern world has achieved over necessity is due to the emancipation of labor, that is, to the fact that the *animal laborans* was permitted to occupy the public realm; and yet, as long as the *animal laborans* remains in possession of it, there can be no true public realm, but only private activities displayed in the open.
>
> (Arendt 1958: 134)

In a consumer society labour is meant to produce goods that generate happiness, and yet this is so insatiable that labour cannot deliver and so produces unhappiness. A futile 'waste economy' has grown, where products 'must be almost as quickly devoured and discarded as they have appeared in the world' (Arendt 1958: 134). Furthermore, such labouring may no longer have the status of labour because:

> the last stage of the laboring society, the society of jobholders, demands of its members a sheer automatic functioning, as though individual life had actually been submerged in the over-all life process of the species and the only active decision still required of the individual

were to let go, so to speak, to abandon his individuality, the still individually sensed pain and trouble of living, and acquiesce in a dazed, 'tranquilized,' functional type of behavior. The trouble with modern theories of behaviorism is not that they are wrong but that they could become true, that they actually are the best possible conceptualization of certain obvious trends in modern society. It is quite conceivable that the modern age – which began with such an unprecedented and promising outburst of human activity – may end in the deadliest, most sterile passivity history has ever known.

(Arendt 1958: 322)

This passivity is part of rendering action and politics as a form of survival (labour) and making (work), and this has been based on the need for security. In Arendt's day security issues focused on the dangers of nuclear war, and now it is the threats to capital accumulation in a globalised economy:

much modern political thought has applied the mentalities and configurations of work, of 'making', to politics with murderous results. Modern discourses and practices of security further assimilate human plurality into a life of meaningless consumption. For Arendt, in contrast, islands of security only survive in the political realm as long as the binding power of mutual promises and agreed purposes keep the political space intact. Political security is fragile and rare, as intangible a political experience as one could possibly imagine.

(Owens 2011: 28)

The passivity identified by Arendt can be seen in schools and has been generated by the formulation and practice of ELMA as labour and action.

Successive UK governments have focused on failure as a key policy strategy in England: schools fail (Gove 2012), headteachers fail (Moorhead 2012), teachers fail (DfEE 1998) and children fail (DfEE 1997). Solutions have been in the form of labour where teaching and learning has been reduced to the delivery and assessment of externally designed classroom packages, where remodelling the school workforce means that qualified teachers do not need to do the delivery. The creation of a data-rich school through targets, testing, inputting and analysing means that professional practice can become work through the crafting of a performance regime, where underachievement is 'smoked out' (DfES 2004a). Studying white and green papers, speeches and legislation shows that this labour and work has been presented as active with the agency of the headteacher as *the* school leader. It seems as if headteachers are to be active and do things and the act of doing is how action is framed. So headteachers must meet national standards in their training and performance (DfES 2004b), establish a vision and a mission for school improvement, and take responsibility for standards and the conduct of staff and students. Being a leader is defined in terms of hierarchy where leadership as a power process is the property of this elite person who is separated from everyone else on the basis of role, remuneration and responsibilities. Even rebranding in the form of distributed leadership still retains the supremacy of the leader-centric structure with a division of labour, with forms of delegation used in order to move work down the production line. Government-commissioned research has been used to support this, with studies examining relationships between headteacher labour and work and student outcomes (Day *et al.* 2009), and functionally descriptive and normative accounts have been made regarding what headteachers need to do to put changes into action (Coles and Southworth 2005). The National College set up in 2000 has not only been central to determining which research can take place and what can be published, but also it has led and controlled training. Importantly, research about the National College shows that it is legally and practically a delivery agency of the government, and so its remit is to control the profession as a means of securing the effective and efficient implementation of reforms locally (Gunter 2012a).

Successive governments have called on and helped to construct a TLP network of intellectuals and empirical researchers who have enabled active ELMA labour and work to be conceptualised, turned into training packages and constantly updated in ways that have been attractive. This has its roots in the school improvement and school effectiveness epistemic groups, where improvement is about change through, for example, technical planning (e.g. Hargreaves and Hopkins 1991), capacity building processes (e.g. Harris and Lambert 2003) and understanding how change happens (e.g. Fullan 2003), and effectiveness is through measuring and predicting (e.g. Sammons *et al.* 1997). The underlying epistemology of this itself is a form of labour (data collection, number crunching) and work (formation of case studies for improvement), and while this field takes action as activity and puts ideas into action, there is no evidence of action in the form of politics. Indeed, debates about ideas and purposes are seen as problematic and potentially vulgar, and contrary to field purposes of supporting policy (Gunter 2012b). While policymakers applaud this (e.g. Barber 2007) it is depoliticised in the form of how to design and deliver in such a way as to implement the required changes. Such knowledge producers present themselves as politically neutral but in reality they are doing political labour and work. They have been close to government through being commissioned to lead on projects, taking up roles in government or its agencies, and giving advice and general support.

However, this is not the type of politics that Arendt argues for. Instead there is an exchange based on a contractual trade relationship: knowledge workers in universities seek access to funded projects and government gains the legitimacy of the university; knowledge workers in business seek access to new markets and government gains the legitimacy of the private sector; and professionals seek access to shaping reforms, and government gains the legitimacy of the profession (Gunter 2012a).

For an Arendtian approach to politics to be in evidence then there would need to be a pluralism of people and ideas in the policy process. The starting point would need to be different, with an emphasis on educational purposes, and so the challenges of being a child (Smyth 2006) and the success of children (Smyth 2011) would need recognition. The challenges of being a teacher (Compton and Weiner 2008) and the success of teachers (Gewirtz *et al.* 2009) would need recognition. The challenges of being a headteacher (Thomson 2009) and the success of headteachers (Winkley 2002) would need recognition. Research that connects adult and student practice in the classroom to the bigger picture of social injustice would need to be in evidence (Apple 2010), and the role of researchers as activists and partners in the change process would need to be central (Anderson 2009). This has its roots in critical approaches where ELMA is conceptualised as a communal and shared resource (e.g. Foster 1986, Smyth 1989), and in particular within policy scholarship where the labour and work of professionals has been identified and charted (e.g. Ball 2003, Gewirtz 2002), and alternative approaches to action in the Arendtian sense have been formulated (e.g. Grace 1995, Ozga 2000a). The underlying epistemology includes labour and work but also politics in the sense of creating spaces where ideas, evidence and strategies can be opened up to scrutiny (e.g. Ball 2007), and new ways of thinking about this through theory and theorising take place (e.g. Ball 1995). Debates about ideas and purposes are central (e.g. Gunter 1997), and the processes involved are recognised as being key to understanding what is known and worth knowing about.

Policymakers are usually irritated by this and can openly oppose (Gunter and Thomson 2006), and do not normally involve those who want to open up debate and consider alternatives to what is on offer. Indeed, these researchers often see themselves as standing outside of the 'knowledge for action' (Hoyle 1986) networks, and see their 'knowledge for understanding' (Hoyle 1986) as a vital contribution. However, it is also clear that a movement between politics and theory, in the way that Young (2008) acknowledges, happens in this part of the field, where the interplay between the two and the distinctiveness of the two is located within professional practice (see also Gunter 2012a). Interestingly Story 5 is a quote from a headteacher who has studied with a leading policy researcher, and Story 6 is based on a partnership between a school and a university school of education where there is a strong policy scholarship community. Politically there is also recognition that schools that seek to develop public realm spaces could be in danger, and so much of this operates under the radar and may not be formally reported. Ironically, Story 5 cannot be followed up as the headteacher took retirement after the officially successful school he led was closed, and Story 6 has been rewritten as Kingswood as a successful school converts to academy status. The dominance of labour and work in the composition and conduct of the workforce, and the fragility of political action in professional practice, is symbolised by these two stories. In the next chapter I go into more depth about the practicalities of how putting changes into action rather than engaging in action can be understood through by using Arendt's (1963) account of the Eichmann trial.

5 Using Arendt to think about ELMA

The *vita contemplativa*

with David Hall, University of Manchester, UK

Introduction

This chapter examines the issue of the subject, particularly the relationship between thinking, judgement and action. This is important at a time when the impact of the dominance of metrics in securing national standards is one of damage to educational processes, particularly teacher and learner dispositions (Galton 2007, Ravitch 2010a). It seems that the workforce and students are ambivalent about schools, with some abandoning them (Butt and Gunter 2007, Smyth 2011), but significantly it is those who stay and who seem to be accepting of destructive modernisation that need to be addressed. Reports from empirical studies will generate examples of educational professionals who have faced tough situations to think through, and this not only raises questions about decision making but also the rationales provided for those decisions. This can be illuminated by Young-Bruehl and Kohn (2001) where they quote from and analyse what Karl Jaspers wrote to Arendt:

> 'what a life you have led, a life given to you and earned by you with a steadfastness that has mastered the evil, the horror that has come from without and ground so many others down'. That is beautifully said and seems almost exactly right. But to 'master' that evil, Arendt had to judge for herself not only those who enacted it, but those who suffered it; and in doing so, she found that what ground them all down did not primarily come 'from without'.
>
> (Young-Bruehl and Kohn: 253)

Written with David Hall, the chapter will report on data from the ESRC-funded project about the social practices of school organisation, and in particular the discourses about and for distributed leadership (Hall *et al.* 2011). Drawing mainly on Arendt's (1963) text, *Eichmann in Jerusalem:*

A Report on the Banality of Evil, the chapter will consider the predicaments when professional practice is determined externally and in ways that are destructive of professionalism and the caring imperative. In doing so we are mindful of the disagreements over Arendt's analysis of the 'banality of evil' and so making it 'one of the most disputed books ever written' (Kohn 2003: xvi). However, as already examined, her analysis of the human condition within totalitarian conditions directs attention to matters of collaboration and resistance, particularly in relation to radical neoliberal and neoconservative educational reform projects such as distributed leadership.

The banality of evil

Eichmann was captured and taken from Argentina to Israel in 1960, where he was put on trial for war crimes, specifically his role in the mass deportation of Jews to Eastern European ghettos and extermination camps. He was found guilty and executed in 1962. Hannah Arendt attended the trial to report for *The New Yorker*, and her account was subsequently published in *Eichmann in Jerusalem: A Report on the Banality of Evil*.

There are three main themes from this analysis on the 'banality of evil' that will be engaged with: first, the 'following orders' defence by Eichmann, and Arendt's analysis of his 'thoughtlessness'; second, the careerism used by Eichmann to position himself; and third, the context in which the holocaust happened, with particular reference to Arendt's identification of collaboration and resistance. All three themes can be recognised within Arendt's (1994) report of Raymond A. Davies' first eyewitness account of Maidanek death camp (Davies was a correspondent for the Jewish Telegraph Agency and broadcaster for the Canadian Broadcasting Corporation):

> Q. Did you kill people in the camp? A. Yes.
> Q. Did you poison them with gas? A. Yes.
> Q. Did you bury them alive? A. It sometimes happened.
> Q. Were the victims picked from all over Europe? A. I suppose so.
> Q. Did you personally help kill people? A. Absolutely not. I was only paymaster in the camp.
> Q. What did you think of what was going on? A. It was bad at first but we got used to it.
> Q. Do you know the Russians will hang you? A. (Bursting into tears) Why should they? *What have I done?* [Italics mine. PM, Sunday, No. 12, 1944]

(Arendt 1994: 127)

Arendt (2003) regarded such accounts as that of a 'desk murderer' (p241), or someone who positioned themselves in a way that seemed to be defendable, but for Arendt these labourers and workers are more guilty than those who committed the physical murdering.

What Arendt did was to give recognition to how evil was done by ordinary people doing ordinary things in extraordinary times. Notably she identified that Eichmann had an 'almost total inability ever to look at anything from the other fellow's point of view' (Arendt 1963: 18), and so 'it was not stupidity but *thoughtlessness*' (Arendt 1978: 4) that mattered. Young-Bruehl (2006) notes that by using the word 'thoughtless' Arendt actually meant 'a mental condition reflecting remoteness from reality, inability to grasp a reality that stares you in the face – a failure of imagination and judgement' (Young-Bruehl 2006: 108). Arendt (1963) provides a fuller explanation:

> for when I speak of the banality of evil, I do so only on the strictly factual level, pointing to a phenomenon which stared one in the face at the trial . . . Except for an extraordinary diligence in looking out for his personal advancement, he had no motives at all. And this diligence in itself was in no way criminal; he certainly would never have murdered his superior in order to inherit his post. He *merely*, put the matter colloquially, *never realized what he was doing*. It was precisely his lack of imagination which enabled him to sit for months on end facing a German Jew who was conducting the police interrogation, pouring out his heart to the man and explaining again and again how it was that he reached only the rank of lieutenant colonel in the SS and that it had not been his fault that he was not promoted.
>
> (Arendt 1963: 114)

What this generates are understandings that making the system work in an efficient and effective way is a reasonable defence:

> Really he had done nothing. He had only carried out orders and since when has it been a crime to carry out orders? Since when has it been a virtue to rebel? Since when could one only be decent by welcoming death? What then had he done?
>
> (Arendt 1994: 127)

Arendt gets underneath this by recognising that genocide is labour and work, and to make it happen 'people must be hired and paid; it is to be done well, they must be supervised and promoted' (Robin 2007: unpaged).

This required 'jobholders' who are also 'good family men' (Arendt 1994: 128), and so Eichmman 'acted not as a man but as a mere functionary whose functions could just as easily have been carried out by anyone else . . . that it was a mere accident that he did it and not somebody else, since after all somebody had to do it' (Arendt 1963: 117). He admired Hitler not because of beliefs and ideas but because he had risen from a lance-corporal to the Fuhrer, and Eichmann would not be blamed for his labour and work because he had not been promoted to the level where such things were decided: 'proving his obedience to his superiors, in other words, was more important to him than demonstrating the flickering of moral conscience' (Bowring 2011: 224). Some 30 years later Arendt (1994: 16) came to the conclusion that 'I was really of the opinion that Eichmann was a buffoon.'

Arendt (1963) identifies the contextual issues in which Eichmann and his like were located. In designing and undertaking his labour and work there are two important issues: first, that genocide does not need violent murderers: 'the trouble with Eichmann was precisely that so many were like him, and that the many were neither perverted nor sadistic, that they were, and still are, terribly and terrifyingly normal' (Arendt 1963: 103); and, second, this labour and work was a duty to be performed: 'as Eichmann told it, the most potent factor in the soothing of his own conscience was the simple fact that he could see no one, no one at all, who actually was against the Final Solution' (Arendt 1963: 60). Arendt (1963) argues that those who designed and delivered the holocaust were not sadists, as such types had been screened out, and many were 'the parasites of the "great" criminals' (Arendt 2003: 253). The Nazi murderers saw what they were doing as 'historic, grandiose, unique' (p45). If they were troubled by their conscience then it was fabricated from 'murder' to 'grant(ing) a mercy death' (p50):

> The trick used by Himmler – who apparently was rather strongly afflicted with these instinctive reactions himself – was very simple and probably very effective; it consisted in turning these instincts around, as it were, in directing them toward the self. So that instead of saying: what horrible things I did to people!, the murderers would be able to say: what horrible things I had to watch in the pursuance of my duties, how heavily the task weighed upon my shoulders!
>
> (p46)

Arendt has been severely criticised for her analysis, for seeming to make out that millions of deaths were normal rather than a crime, and yet Arendt's contribution is just this, that she showed that terrible things can

be done on a day to day basis, that people can and do calculate and coop-
erate: 'the problem, the personal problem, was not what our enemies did
but what our friends did' (Arendt 1994: 10–11). As people disappeared
from work places and homes, and children from school desks, it seems
there were no public protests. Consciences could be kept clear by the
political use of categories of Jews who were deported because they were
Polish rather than German, or who had failed to fight in the First World
War compared with those who had. Arendt (1963: 42) concluded 'that
conscience as such had apparently got lost in Germany', and she presents
an interesting example of this:

> The best proof, if proof were still needed, of the extent to which the
> whole people, regardless of party affiliation and direct implication,
> believed in the 'new order' for no other reason than that was the way
> things were, was perhaps the incredible remark Eichmann's lawyer,
> who had never belonged to the Nazi Party, made twice during the trial
> in Jerusalem, to the effect that what had happened in Auschwitz and
> the other extermination camps had been 'a medical matter'. It was as
> though morality, at the very moment of its total collapse within an old
> and highly civilised nation, stood revealed in the original meaning of
> the word, as a set of *mores*, of customs and manners, which could be
> exchanged for another set with no more trouble than it would take to
> change the table manners of a whole people.
>
> (Arendt 2003: 43)

In addition to this, Arendt examined the way the Jewish community
handled the holocaust, and in doing so shifted the analysis, because the
question to be addressed is not 'why did you obey?' but 'why did you
support?' (Arendt 2003: 48). She tells the story of how this happened:

> The Jewish Councils of Elders were informed by Eichmann or his men
> of how many Jews were needed to fill each train, and they made out
> the list of deportees. The Jews registered, filled out innumerable forms,
> answered pages and pages of questionnaires regarding their property
> so that it could be seized the more easily; they then assembled at the
> collection points and boarded the trains. The few who tried to hide or
> to escape were rounded up by a special Jewish police force. As far as
> Eichmann could see, no one protested, no one refused to cooperate.
> *'Immerzu fahren hier die Leute zu ihrem eigenen Begräbnis'* (Day in day out
> the people here leave for their own funeral), as a Jewish observer put it
> in Berlin in 1943.
>
> (Arendt 1963: 58)

Arendt (1963) argues that there were a few who had a conscience and who opposed Hitler, and who refused the oath and so lost their elite posts, and those who helped Jews. But she sadly concludes that even if a person does not agree or accept what is taking place, the quiet disappearance of people and the lives surrounding them (shops, children in school) means that standing up and fighting can become meaningless. It was in her later work on political action as distinct from labour and work (Arendt 1958), and her *Life of the Mind* (Arendt 1978), that generated the optimism that total-itarian conditions need not crystallise into totalitarianism and that human beings can do something new:

> Arendt remained determined to shed light on the peculiar way that humans, tempted by the promise that 'anything is possible', appeared so willing to exchange their freedom for the absolute omnipotence of inhuman forces. This, for Arendt, was a test of her own powers of political judgement, which in her definition must refuse to subsume the distinctive features of a historical event under pre-existing classifi-cations, trends or laws.
>
> (Bowring 2011: 232–233)

For Arendt the question to be pursued is about how thinking is not only a political process, but is also solitary, where people need to withdraw (Duarte 2001) because thinking 'is the sensation of being alive' (Arendt 1978: 197). The relationship with action is central: 'thinking is always out of order, interrupts all ordinary activities and is interrupted by them' (Arendt 1978: 197). In addition to this Arendt asks about the power of this thinking as central to moral issues:

> could the activity of thinking as such, the habit of examining whatever happens to come to pass or to attract attention, regardless of results and specific content, could this activity be among the conditions that make men abstain from evil-doing or even actually 'condition' them against it?
>
> (Arendt 1978: 5)

In this sense it is the *vita contemplativa* along with the *vita activa* where the conditions for action and freedom, or for totalitarianism and banality, can emerge.

We now intend moving on to use this analysis to think about school leadership in England as a means of not only contributing to this national field but also of generating analysis that speaks to other systems. In doing so we are presenting an analysis prompted by putting side by side Arendt's account of knowledge production with that of our account of what is happening in public services education. In doing so we recognise the distinctiveness of then and now, but also we expose striking similarities that are sufficient to warrant our close and serious attention, and are saying something compelling that needs to be opened up for scrutiny and debate. Located both simultaneously inside and outside of this, we intend to examine what seems to be ordinary, but on closer inspection could be dangerously extraordinary. Public services education is in a precarious situation in England, and following Arendt we are taking our responsibilities seriously as a way of trying to understand that everything – notably the destruction of public services education – is possible. Our intentions are to bring into the open the conditions that suggest totalitarian tendencies, and that there are seemingly normal processes at work that are doing abnormal things. As Bernstein (1997) argues, what is being struggled for by Arendt (1963) is comprehension 'even when what we encounter appears to be thoroughly incomprehensible' (Bernstein 1997: 298). Arendt's methodology enables us to unsettle the attention given to improving schools through privatisation, and refocus instead on the purposes of education for all. We know this is painful, but we also know that people are angry at what is taking place. In essence, when the question is asked, 'What were you thinking and doing when they took away our schools and our teachers?' we hope that we are and will be participating in the current movement to renew and rebuild them.

The banality of leadership

Policy scholarship has identified the damaging impact of simultaneous and incoherent centralisation and decentralisation on education and professionals (e.g. Whitty *et al.* 1998), with recognition of the dangers of the dramatic and intensive turn towards leadership (e.g. Ozga 2000b). However, a different type of analysis is needed if we are to uncover the trends and tendencies within everyday practices. Arendt's analysis of the conditions for totalitarianism based on labour and action combined with thoughtlessness generates the possibility that ELMA is on one level banal and on another may illuminate the banality of evil. These are serious matters. We are not the first to raise them, as Samier (2008) has identified 'passive evil' within the ELMA field where: 'the danger lies not so much in individual perpetrators, but in others who avoid responding out of fear or moral blindness' (Samier 2008: 5). Such an approach is evident in the literatures where there are accounts of thoughtlessness and passive evil in responding to neoliberal and neoconservative education projects that have enabled totalitarian conditions to be visible and to begin to crystallise.

Such accounts are about major policy reforms (e.g. Beckett 2007, Coffield and Williamson 2012, Gunter 2011), about headteachers (Grace 1995), about teachers (Gunter and Hall 2012) and about children (Fielding 2006). In addition to this there is evidence of how intellectual work has been used in ways that support totalitarian tendencies, and how governments draw upon and create intellectual communities in education in order to support what are labelled as modernising reforms (Gunter 2012a).

ELMA is replete with examples of banality: first, where professionals seek to mediate destructive policies by sifting, interpreting and fudging, and pragmatically respond to the situation they are in and/or have imaginings of how the situation may unfold that can advantage or disadvantage; second, where professionals protect and advance their careers through cooperation, and are given a leadership identity located in thoughtless standards; and third, where professionals seek out opportunities from the new reforms, and at most engage in 'decaf resistance' (Page 2011: 2) and as such give an impression of agency but in reality maintain established power relations.

ELMA is replete with examples of banal research: first, projects that focus on either policy science measurement and technical implementation and/or present normative claims for a better world based on neoliberal/ neoconservative beliefs glossed over with selected data or examples; second, projects that are commissioned by organisations that are concerned to deliver neoliberal/neoconservative reforms, which frame research remits and require approved of findings; and third, projects that focus on collaboration with improvement and effectiveness in ways that are disconnected from an examination of the polity, and are forms of 'espresso resistance' (Page 2011: 2) where robust dissent and opposition are eschewed.

TLP is banal in its emphasis on motivating processes decorated with logos and soundbites rather than educational ideas and values, and has the potential for evil because it creates the conditions where alternatives are not allowed, and fabricates modernisation that enables dismantling and marketisation rather than the reform and renewal of public services. ELMA has been more actively involved in TLP than in developing alternatives, and so has tended to popularise and indeed locate within the TLP networks. Challenging the fantasy school within TLP has had to come from outside of mainstream ELMA, where critical and socially critical work, such as this book series, continues to address some serious matters.

In order to illustrate this we intend to focus on the rise of distributed leadership as a form of improved professional practice and funded research projects. In doing this we draw on data and analysis from the ESRCfunded Distributed Leadership and the Social Practices of School Organisation (SPSO) project (RES-000-22-3610) (Hall *et al.* 2011). In this study we examined the evidence base for distributed leadership, and within five case study schools we focused on the discursive construction and explanations of leadership practices through interviews, observations and Q sorts (see Gunter *et al.* 2013, Hall *et al.* 2012).

Our main findings from this project are:

Policy context: a study of policy texts shows that distributed leadership is an officially endorsed model of good leadership practice internationally (e.g. Huber *et al.* 2007). This can be observed in England in the form of dedicated web page provision with case study evidence at the National College, through to official policy texts (e.g. Hopkins 2001) and speeches (e.g. Munby 2006) that confirm its importance to securing high standards. Investment in building an evidence base continues with literature reviews (e.g. Bennett *et al.* 2003b), empirical projects (e.g. MacBeath *et al.* 2004) and by individual professionals (e.g. Lloyd 2005). At the time of the New Labour governments (1997–2010) the promotion of distributed leadership tended to be done more by the National College than the Department (Gunter 2012a), where it has been configured as a hybrid of transformational leadership. The primacy of the single leader remains, but effectiveness and efficiency can be enhanced through processes of distribution and job redesign.

Evidence base: a study of the literatures with reports of distributed leadership has generated categories that show knowledge claims to be: first, functionally descriptive where distribution is at work, and functionally normative where the lack of a robust evidence base does not stop advocacy; second, critically focused on the realities of the job regarding how habits and ways of working get the job done; and third, socially critical where leadership is a communal resource rather than the property of an elite person who distributes it to others. Our analysis shows the dominance of functional descriptive and normative knowledge claims, and how this relates to the working of the leadership industry (Gunter 2012a, Gunter *et al.* 2013).

Case study schools: the officially prescribed model of functional and normatively appropriate distributed leadership was found to be inscribed within the professional identities of research participants. In some schools the institutional logic was tightly tied to the delivery of externally defined outcomes and there was a strong association with forms of leadership that were highly controlling and regulative. In such contexts the development of professional identities was largely emasculated by attempts to create conforming professionals closely identifying their work with the tightly defined aims of the school, and discourses of distribution were frequently superficial yet highly affirmative. Identity emasculation of a different kind was evident in schools where demands for professional conformism were less marked and where discourses of distributed leadership and institutional logics were tied both to the delivery of externally defined outcomes and to notions of professional autonomy. In such schools distributed leadership was frequently imbued with strong personal and institutional meanings, but within settings that could offer strictly limited affordances for the enactment of such meanings. Resistance to the notion of distributed leadership was also evident amongst teachers not recognising themselves as senior leaders in these schools. This took various forms including outright rejection of and scepticism towards the possibilities for the application of distributed leadership in their institutions.

It seems to us that distributed leadership is a benign, seductive and exciting label for the giving and following of orders. It is an elite discourse, but as it speaks to traditional professional cultures of collegiality it can be used to mimic ways of thinking and doing that are already accepted. It is part of a process identified in the business sector regarding the way force and consent operate through everyday practices (see, for example, Buraway 1979). So thoughtlessness about distributed leadership is located in assumptions about fit with how things are done anyway, and a failure to think about the reality of how it is being used. While the rhetoric focuses on the limitations of the autonomous transformational leader together with recognition of the reality and necessity of others being involved in running a school, it seems that careerism dominates. Remodelling the school workforce includes creating opportunities for headteachers to be out of school working with other schools to improve standards (for example, as executive heads) or heading up federations and other forms of organisational collaborations and chains of schools. Work has to be passed down the line to others who do labour and work, which is officially known as leadership but in reality is it getting on with the job? This is a means of protecting and enhancing national standards as official data, and so careerism (particularly not losing your job) and extending the pool from which the next generation of heads comes from is a clear policy strategy (see Butt and Gunter 2007). Distributed leadership is based on impression management with claims of agency but in reality empowerment is based on compliance with those who have secured the status that gives them the legitimacy to make decisions about professional practice.

We have examined this by reading our data through models of trust, where we argue that the realities of distributed leadership are based on deception (Gunter and Hall 2012). So at one school a system of what is called 'dispersed leadership' is used as a means of enabling all staff to be involved in discussing the detail of, as opposed to the nature of, policy changes. Specifically those working at the school cannot complain that they have not been asked if they find a change uncongenial, and our data show an acceptance of this, where dissent illuminates that teachers and other staff recognise what is going on but this does not translate into opposition. At a second school the continued dominance of the headteacher is also illustrated, where the redesign of the leadership structure was based on the need to deal with an inherited financial crisis combined with securing headteacher control over classroom practice. There is an overt commitment to distributed leadership, and again while the staff are somewhat cynical they have not challenged this. Notably, the careerism of the headteacher is key where he planned to use the distribution of responsibility to enable him to be an executive headteacher.

Just two examples illustrate the structural and cultural ways in which banal leadership strategies are enacted within schools: distributed leadership claims to do things differently and in ways that modernise the profession, and so it is attractive, but at the same time it is recognised as a rebranding of delegation and so it fits with established hierarchies and cultures. It enables the 'onion' (Arendt 2006a) structure to work, where the 'will of the fuhrer' can permeate thinking and doing. It provides a drama (script, methods and improvised know how) that can be staged by those who are already advantaged. Attendance at the National College (either on line or in person) means that those designated as leaders never hear any alternatives to the labour and work that they are exhorted and compelled to do. Followers are rebranded as leaders; for some this is an exciting opportunity, and for others it can be dealt with through ignoring what is going on as long as it does not interfere with classroom practice.

What troubles us is the interrelationship between macro totalitarian conditions and the realities of what happens in a school. Arendt requires researchers to ask themselves what is new about a situation. In doing this we would both like to argue that what is new about the current configuration and distribution of distributed leadership is: first, how crystallisation of totalitarian conditions is enforced through the shift from NPM to New Public Leadership (NPL), which speaks inclusively but actually is making particular people (professionals and children) superfluous; and second, how those enacting this locally may do so on the basis that distributed leadership is full of good intentions, is good for the soul and is what they (and not others) genuinely want within professional practice, but they are thoughtless about the realities of such functionality. We now intend to illuminate these points through examining the interrelationship between

NPL and a case study school, where our intention, following Hartley (2007), is to open up the brutality that is veiled by the effervescence of distributed leadership. In doing so we are mindful of a paraphrased Arendtian question: when was it ever a crime to meet OfSTED requirements? We will come back to this at the end of the chapter.

The banality of distributed leadership

The modernisation of the education sector offers an opportunity to examine aspects of Arendt's work in a contemporary context that although far removed from the horrors of the Final Solution nevertheless offers important insights into the workings of organisations and the behaviours of individuals caught up in political events that can appear for some, at least, to offer little choice but a banal conformity. By examining evidence from the SPSO project (Hall *et al.* 2011) in regard to Arendt's arguments about the banality of evil we seek to highlight the continuing salience of Arendt's work and to illuminate those ways in which her contribution to knowledge continues to provoke and disturb.

Public sector educational provision has been subject to a process of permanent revolution (Pollitt, 1990) as part of the New Public Management (NPM); the 'dominant paradigm' (McLaughlin *et al.* 2002) for public management in North America, Australasia, the Pacific Rim, the UK and parts of Scandinavia. NPM is typically characterised by a clear preference for markets and competition, a marked promotion of private sector styles of management and the use of explicit performance measures and standards (Clarke and Newman 1997, McLaughlin *et al.* 2002). In England NPM emerged under the Thatcher governments (1979-1990) and has continued under subsequent governments in various forms for in excess of 30 years.

NPM related reforms within the education sector in England have tightly matched the generic features of this development referred to above. Foremost amongst these have been the creation of national and, in some countries, regional standardised testing systems marginalising or displacing previous systems of assessment, an accompanying and dramatically enhanced emphasis upon measuring pupil, teacher and school performance and the development of educational quasi-markets (Le Grand and Bartlett 1993) in which schools compete with one another as business units. This much changed educational landscape has been locally overseen within schools and other educational institutions by a remodelled cadre of managers with a marked emphasis upon managerialist practices (Gewirtz 2002) producing 'governing data' (Ozga 2009). Proponents of NPM within the education sector seek to create new remodelled public service provision that more closely resembles their notions of efficiency and effectiveness. This remodelling process, closely associated with education imagined as a packaged commodity to be delivered to its consumers, most accurately represented by the notion of deliverology (Barber 2007), has had fundamentally important implications for schools and other educational institutions. This is primarily on account of the requirement placed upon such institutions to become repositories of this new approach to education with far-reaching and deep implications for those studying and working within them. It goes beyond the scope of this chapter to itemise such effects upon different individuals and groups caught up in this modernisation programme, but as well as evidence pointing to the tight grip that this new managerialism has exerted upon the education sector, there is now widespread evidence of the damage done to young people through their exposure to regimes of testing from young ages, not least in terms of invitations to imagine themselves as failures well before they reach the secondary phase of their education (Reay and William 1999). For those working within schools stress and burnout (Troman and Woods 2001), the intensification of work (Hargreaves 2003) and the terror that they have experienced when faced with a relentlessly performative working environment (Ball 2003) have all been identified as problems besetting teachers and others working within this remodelled sector. Yet despite the identification of these and other related problems, not least the debilitating effects of working with constant 're-disorganisation' (Pollitt 2007), NPM has continued to be relentlessly pursued within many educational contexts and has frequently been accompanied by claims of improvement and positive change often linked to measured changes in standards of educational attainment.

One particular feature of NPM has been the emergence of leadership or 'leaderism' as a key dimension of the reform process (O'Reilly and Reed 2010), and it is to this particular hybrid development in NPM within the context of educational reform that this chapter now attends. While NPM created the fantasy of the technically perfect school, the functional and normative leadership researchers bought into this and developed it in ways that could deliver neoliberal and neoconservative goals of dismantling public education. For example, Leithwood *et al.* (1999) draw on school effectiveness to engage in discussions about leadership values that are integral to securing the school as a 'high reliability organisation' (HRO) (p213), where just as the public would not tolerate, for example, regular airline failure, then they should not accept school or learner failure:

> Application to schools of the full set of HRO characteristics would result in an organization with many of the structural features of a traditional school but with, for example, more flexible, varied and

> task-dependent sets of professional relationships; greater commitment
> by staff to a clearer and more precisely focused set of goals; much
> greater attention to evidence about the effects of teaching practices;
> and meticulous attention to the maintenance of the equipment and
> technology considered important for achieving the instructional
> purposes of the school.
>
> (Leithwood *et al.* 1999: 214)

This emphasis on non-educational process and values enabled leadership to
be integrated into both getting the job done better and doing it in ways
that emotionally feels like making a difference to organisational outcomes.
Research by Leithwood and colleagues has been highly influential internationally and certainly in England (e.g. Leithwood *et al.* 1999), and it
brought the notion that identified leaders in schools would be agents of
NPM related change within a modernising environment. Initially school
headteachers as the transformative and imagined heroic single leaders of
their schools were the target of this discursive intervention into the NPM
process. Within this headteachers were invited to view themselves as
agents of change, playing a key role in the modernisation of schooling. In
England headteachers were actively courted through a variety of means
including the creation of a specialist National College, the feting of individual 'super-heads' through the honours system and a widening pay gap
with classroom teachers. Subsequently this discourse of leadership for a
variety of reasons, not least the apparent failure of single leadership, came
to be more widely dispersed amongst a wider community of those working
in the education sector. This was through the introduction of the so-called
distributed leadership, where leadership was to be spread throughout
organisations, with all working (and in some versions studying) in schools
invited to view themselves as leaders as a form of 'total leadership'
(Leithwood *et al.* 2006). This process of spreading leadership from those
hierarchically privileged individuals, mainly headteachers, to teachers,
middle managers, support staff and children in schools can be viewed as an
audacious act whereby the cultural ideology of leadership was made available to a vastly increased range of education workers in order to secure
increased support for the reform process. While autocracy in school leadership is not new (see Grace 1995), what is new is how hierarchy has had a
'make-over' through the use of the language of participation and inclusion.
The identification and use of 'public value' arguments has helped with
this, whereby those occupying public roles can present their work as active
in the public sphere (e.g. Benington and Moore 2011), particularly through
how leadership of the organisation is being linked to social entrepreneurship with business and philanthropy (Sandler 2010).

The SPSO project sought to better understand the process whereby distributed leadership had rapidly become the approved form of leadership in schools within a wider environment tightly controlled through a range of NPM related reforms. The research was conducted in five schools with the intention of developing deeper understandings of the perceptions of teachers, headteachers and others working in schools in relation to leadership and distributed leadership. Given the stark contradictions between the managerial intent of NPM with its narrow, relentless focus upon measured standards of attainment in education and the agential connotations of leadership we might have anticipated our research revealing widespread scepticism or even hostility towards distributed leadership within the teaching profession. This would be consistent with a wide range of previous research pointing to the tensions experienced by teachers as they were required to shift from teaching identities firmly associated with the care and nurturing of children within a welfarist model of educational provision to those associated with the new performative NPM environment with its relentless emphasis upon test results (e.g. Helsby 1999). Instead what our research revealed was largely the opposite (Hall *et al.* 2011): a strong and widespread identification with the idea of, but not necessarily knowledge about the label of, distributed leadership. In what follows we use Arendt's thinking to understand how, within one of the schools, this identification with distributed leadership can be explained within a wider environment dominated by NPM/L related reforms.

At Birch Tree School, a secondary school for 11-18 year olds in an urban environment in the north of England, it became clear early on in our research that the headteacher, Simon, was a highly influential, dominant and controlling figure within the institution. For a variety of reasons, not least the highly demanding performance targets established for Birch Tree set against the school's pupils coming from some of the most socio-economically disadvantaged homes in the district of the city where it was located, this was a school where the pressures to meet the NPM related institutional performance targets were likely to have been experienced particularly intensely. This is one account primarily of the immense difficulties facing schools serving socio-economically disadvantaged chidren when they attempt to secure marked increases in standards of measured attainment (Raffo *et al.* 2010).

Evidence collected at Birch Tree clearly pointed to the predominance of a top-down, hierarchical organisational model in which Simon played a commanding role: 'I get paid a lot of money and the reason I get paid a lot of money is because the buck stops here' (Simon, headteacher). This is recognised by staff, for example:

'[Simon] rules with an iron fist.'

(class teacher)

'We have, obviously, the Principal at the top and he dictates, dictate is probably the wrong word, he helps decide on how the organisation will move forward.'

(class teacher)

Simon's dominant role at Birch Tree was also accompanied by a marked absence of dissent where there is compliance with hierarchy:

'People don't tend to say they are unhappy . . . because sometimes they are concerned about repercussions.'

(middle leader)

'Generally when people have been here a while and have adjusted to the way things work, I think people are content, having said that, people who aren't content usually move on pretty quickly.'

(lead practitioner)

In addition to this, there are attempts to suppress actual debate in the life of the school:

'If you are not seen as being supportive on school policies and you are not supporting the school ethos, it doesn't really look very good.'

(middle leader)

'There has been a time when people have passed comment and it's got back and they've got into trouble about it.'

(middle leader)

This intolerance of dissent, and even what might be regarded as professional debate, was also made clear by Simon who was very upfront about his approach to fellow professionals who did not match up to his standards:

'I absolutely 100% knew that I was not taking all them shit people out of the predecessor schools . . . I wasn't prepared to have them because I know that if you give me two rusty sheds at the bottom of the garden and excellent people, I'll give you a school.'

(Simon, headteacher)

It was interesting therefore for us to find that claims of distributed leadership were widespread within Birch Tree. Not only Simon but others participating in our research testified to the existence of distributed leadership and simultaneously expressed the view that they had autonomy. In reviewing the data from research participants drawn from various points in the school hierarchy it became clear to us that they believe that leadership is exercised by staff at a variety of different levels and that distributed leadership is practised at Birch Tree. They also consider that leadership is fundamental to a teacher's job and that it is important that teachers have ownership of decisions made in school. Staff feel confident that they are capable of taking on more leadership responsibility and don't feel that they require training in order to take on a leadership role. It seems that traditional hierarchy and onion structures speak to each other at Birch Tree, where the will of the leader is secured through everyday practices.

Evident within this view of the school is an inability or unwillingness on the part of those working at Birch Tree to consider the seemingly glaring contradictions between the repressive and controlling manner in which Simon was organising school life and the view that leadership had been distributed affording autonomy to teachers. From this perspective there is a clear sense of thoughtlessness that emerges from the responses of our research participants. How can they be so seemingly willing to overlook these contradictions? What is it that enables them to tolerate the controlling and sometimes repressive aspects of organisational life at Birch Tree seemingly without complaint? This sense of thoughtlessness was further underlined by the way in which research participants unfailingly spoke with enthusiasm about the school, their work and what they believe is being achieved there.

In part this thoughtlessness can be explained by the way that Simon has interpreted distributed leadership at Birch Tree in a manner that enabled the reconciliation of this term with his way of running the school: 'Distributed leadership is everybody knowing that they've a place in leadership and what to do. They are guardians of the mission and ethos and that actually they are an important cog in the wheel' (Simon, headteacher). Here we can see how the version of distributed leadership imported into Birch Tree is one where those working at the school are invited to view themselves as 'cogs' in a larger machine. In this way the agential elements of leadership have been combined with the mechanics of cogs and wheels to create a form of highly instrumental and idiosyncratic distributed leadership (Hall *et al.* 2012). This notion of distributed leadership therefore can be viewed as creating the discursive space which enables teachers at Birch Tree to represent repression as autonomy and control as agency. It is a notion of distributed leadership that can be viewed as inviting thoughtlessness, but as a discursive device it is perhaps not sufficiently powerful to explain the degree and extent of thoughtlessness associated with its acceptance.

A further explanation for what we discovered at Birch Tree can be found within the careerism of many of those working there. The sense of satisfaction in working at Birch Tree reported to us cohered around a strong perception of being part of a successful institution where staff talents are recognised and rewarded. In part this can be viewed as being tied to a complimentary report from OfSTED and some increases in the levels of student attainment in national tests, but it was also intimately tied to the related sense that Birch Tree was a very promising school in which to develop your career: 'I think the leadership here is really good, it's the way you feel very supported and very managed in a good way, in a safe way that you are given the opportunities to further your career which in many schools you wouldn't' (teacher). This, from a younger and newer teacher at the school, can be interpreted as speaking to the fears of many new entrants to the teaching profession of working in a school where a large number of pupils are drawn from socio-economically disadvantaged backgrounds. Such schools have long struck fear into the hearts of new teachers on account of lurid tales of errant pupil behaviour that frequently echo down the corridors of teacher education institutes and more privileged schools. Birch Tree offered a reassuring environment within which this teacher felt safe and supported. However, there is also a sense of career opportunities unavailable in other schools. Here the teacher is referring to the status of the school in relation to its capacity to meet NPM targets and the expectation that Birch Tree would be acclaimed for its achievements in this respect. This sense of career advancement linked to working at Birch Tree surfaced when an emerging leader questioned about his understanding of distributed leadership invoked the opportunities and possibilities it afforded in relation to members of staff lower down in the school hierarchy gaining promotion:

> It is an effective form of leadership I think because it's two fold because if you've got people like myself trying to work their way up the leadership ladder, in order to experience how to get to next levels you've got to get access to the types of things that they're doing and the type of things that they're involved in and distributing work as well as leadership efforts . . . I think it's important to allow people who are lower down on the leadership rungs access to these types of things in order to progress themselves.

Here the the prime lens through which distributed leadership is viewed is that of career advancement. Attempts to reflect upon distributed leadership or leadership at Birch Tree more generally were overlooked in favour of an assessment of its potential to develop a career.

The notion that working at the school might help to develop careers was also directly referred to by more senior leaders at the school and was frequently linked Simon's ambitions for the school:

'In terms of the talent and emerging talent, absolutely, Simon is very good at spotting people's potential and skills and using them and I always feel when talking to Simon that he is committed not just to developing leadership for the academy here but also wider and at national level and he does contribute at a national level and he sees part of his role here as growing people so that they can contribute at that level as well.'

(lead practitioner)

'Simon is very much about building capacity, he wants to build a capacity for and expansion of looking after other schools in whatever form that might be, so he wants to know if people can step up from middle leader level to senior level, so he wants to facilitate that and I'm going to make sure that what I do enhances that but also enhances what we do here in driving through improvement basically.'

(vice-principal)

The career ambition in terms of moving upwards in the hierarchy of the teaching profession is transparent here as it is elsewhere. In our view it is directly related to the willingness to tolerate Simon's authoritarian and sometimes repressive regime. In order to 'get on' or 'survive' in this organisation it is necessary to be viewed as supportive of Simon and other powerful members of the leadership team and it is potentially dangerous, in career terms at least, to be challenging ideas such as distributed leadership that have been approved in a public manner. In this sense the teachers script their identity in relation to others who didn't make it from the predecessor schools when academy conversion took place, or who have not stayed long in the new school if they did not fit. This discourse is very strong in our data and it seems that all are potentially superfluous, and there is a survivor narrative at play regarding those who stay. In this way we can see how the conditions have emerged at Birch Tree for professionals to ignore that which they might otherwise find intolerable, working within an autocratic and controlling institution dominated by the need to meet extremely demanding performance targets in a wider environment linked to NPM. The reasons for this thoughtlessness can be located, we believe, within the way in which career success has come to occupy so much professional space.

A final and necessary point is that discussion and decision making is located in very narrowly defined labour and work: the teachers labour to produce OfSTED-ready data and they work to create a form of leadership that stablises their careers and constructs the necessary labour. In Arendtian terms this labour and work prevents pluralism, and for us the issue is not whether there is or is not resistance, but that our respondents found it necessary to make the benefits of the unitary leadership strategy clear with no narratives about how they have engaged in active debates and agreements. Following Scott (1998) the professionals at Birch Tree are 'seeing like a state' where they categorise and seek to know through numbers, or allow themselves to be aggregated in this way. Related to this is our earlier Arendtian-influenced question: when was it ever a crime to meet OfSTED requirements? Technically it is not a crime, and we are not advocating breaking the law. The points we want to make are not new, as Wallace (2001) shows there are dangers involved in distribution when the public accountability system means that, as Thomson (2009) shows, heads are literally on the block. Indeed Gronn's work on the dangers of 'designer leadership' (Gronn 2003) with a one size fits all model juxtaposed with his empirical work on the realities of how professionals actually go about doing their work together, leads him to conclude that the best way to think about leadership is through a 'hybrid leadership mix' where formal leadership is not jettisoned in favour of distributed notions, but instead the two are always in play (Gronn 2009). It seems to us that while research is providing evidence of the realities of how NPM/L is playing out locally, this is not being actively researched in ELMA, and the official accounts of distributed leadership are denying professionals access to other ways of thinking about professional practice. So what we want to raise here is how the thinking that has been done so far in this text shows how power processes are being used to suture together and enable the conditions in which totalitarianism can crystallise, and the very people who are seemingly included as leaders, doing leading and exercising leadership are rendering themselves and others as superfluous. As we write Lepkowska (2012) has just reported about how newly qualified teachers who cannot respond quickly to the standards agenda are being dispensed with, where one former teacher tells the story that: 'within three weeks of starting in September, I was told by a senior member of staff that I was "useless", even though she had not observed me teaching' (Lepkowska 2012: 34). It seems that what is actually being distributed is fear and risk, where the jobs of senior leaders are dependent on the right type of data delivery.

Alternative forms of distributed leadership are evident in the literatures where schools located in socio-economic conditions equivalent to, or worse than, Birch Tree think politically about educational purposes and engage in school redesign that speaks to democratic participation and place-based curricula (see Gandin and Apple 2003, Thomson 2010). Here the emphasis is on educational leadership, where professionals with children and communities actively lead an approach to pedagogy that enables access to high standards, but do so in ways that provoke thinking and action about the ways in which advantage and disadvantage work. At Birch Tree, teachers are labouring very hard to improve the end of school credentials and work ready behaviours of the children, but in doing so they are positioning children as the objects of neoliberal and neoconservative projects. This is not the form of teacher responsibility that Arendt talks about, as she wants teachers to enable children to understand the world they have been born into and have the opportunity do something different. The inherent danger here is that children at Birch Tree learn to perform as compliant workers: so that there is no recognition of the actuality and potentiality of natality at this school.

There is a catastrophe unfolding here; it is not one of standards or a failure to comply with the three-part lesson plan, but seems to be located in compliance and delivery. There is a tendency to deny collective memories or wipe them out through combining radical restructuring of schools with the early promotion of those who have not shared or been trained to access professional histories. Now as reader you may be able to quote data and examples of other schools that are very different to the case we have given, and indeed we have both undertaken research in schools that do have and encourage space for activism. However, our argument is that we need to know what it looks and feels like for spaces to be closed and for people not to look for them. We have heard and been audience to far too many comments, such as, 'just tell me what to do and I will do it', 'it's not in the national curriculum and so I can't do it', and 'OfSTED does not allow that'. We are aware that those who are creating this culture have attacked it through claiming that the profession has been given guidance rather than regulation, or more recently that teachers need to be given freedoms, but in reality free schools are opening without trained teachers. We would want to take seriously Arendt's arguments about taking action rather than labouring and working, and this has to begin with taking advantage of the spaces that do exist to begin to talk about educational purposes. Indeed, we have heard and been audience to comments that generate hope, such as, 'we need as a profession to take back teaching and learning', and 'we should not allow OfSTED to stop us doing what we regard is right and proper'. At a time when politics seems out of reach and politics with a big P is discredited, there may be opportunities for local changes that could make a difference.

It seems that while modernisation is packaged in such a way as being in the interests of children, and that some children do improve their test results, it is clear that decisions about questions of right and wrong are unclear, and we are aware that professionals are making difficult decisions in hard times. And, while we would agree with Arendt (1963) that it is 'cruel and silly' to ask why they didn't protest, we would want to note that the moral conscience displayed by some professionals who do speak out has not so far triggered a profession-wide response. Indeed those who do speak out, such as Greenfield (1978) did in the 1970s, and more recently Barker (2010), can find themselves publicly villified (see Greenfield and Ribbins 1993, Gunter and Fitzgerald 2011). Birch Tree enables the brutality of this to be opened up to scrutiny, and in ways that challenge knowledge claims and production processes. As already shown in this book there are examples of such productive work taking place, and our analysis suggests an urgency for engagement, not least because the unthinkable is unfolding in front of us.

6   Thinking with and against Arendt

Introduction

This book seeks to make a contribution by actively thinking through the current predicaments created by the dominance of the TLP in ELMA using Arendt's methods and conceptual tools. In reaching this stage in this project I remain mindful of the situation that I began with regarding how Arendt is read and used:

> There is one oddity about her current standing, however, which is that in spite of the attention her writings have attracted, they have been little understood. The critical literature contains an unusually high proportion of attacks on positions that, arguably, she did not in fact hold.
>
> (Canovan 1995: 2)

In addition to this, much of her thinking and analysis may not have been recorded:

> Arendt did not make great efforts to communicate her ideas. As she once explained in an interview, the motive behind her work was her own desire to understand, and writing was part of the process of understanding. If this meant that others shared her insights, that was a satisfaction to her, but she suggested half-seriously that if she been blessed with a good enough memory to be able to remember all her thoughts without working them out on paper, she might never have written anything.
>
> (Canovan 1995: 2)

With these points in mind, in this chapter I intend characterising the dilemmas for ELMA, where I focus in particular on gender as a problematic practice and research issue. In doing this I give recognition to critical debates about Arendt's work in regard to two main areas: first, the 'social', and second, the 'boomerang thesis'. These debates about Arendt's thinking and contribution open up questions of the under-developed nature of some of her analysis, along with how potential contradictions have been exposed. However, my overall argument is that her historical and political thinking enables some new insights to be made in regard to ELMA, and I complete the book by relating the analysis to the wider social sciences; specifically I argue that Arendt's oeuvre continues to speak to today's political issues, and may be mobilised for researching knowledge production.

Thinking with Arendt

The reality of life in educational organisations at a time of rapid and ill thought through neoliberal and neoconservative modernisation projects is complex; the most up to date studies show an ongoing struggle by educational professionals against incoherence and contradiction:

> Policy then cannot be reduced to an algorithm (iterations, community, learning, influence or whatever) but also the school cannot be reduced to policy. What comes across in our analysis is school as a creaky social assemblage, that is continually re-validated and under-pinned and moved on by the various efforts of networks of social actors with disparate but more or less focused interests and commitment.
>
> (Ball *et al.* 2012: 70)

However, the colonisation of the ELMA field by the TLP is producing rational control 'algorithmic' models accompanied by exhortations for new and innovative professional practice which defibrillates hearts and sedates minds into approved of labour (and some work). Thinking with, through and against Arendt's historical and political concepts and methods makes a distinctive contribution to understanding and explaining this, through revealing the conditions for totalitarianism, but at the same time by examining events in ways that enable questions to be asked about how the contemporary situation may or may not be crystallising into a totalitarian regime. It is necessary to focus on how interventions into schools through external policy is about removing the spaces for action, and how the job of those locally is to provide a veil of ordered compliance. At the same time analysis shows how there are challenges and resistance to such processes, and how the job of the researcher is not only to open up to scrutiny the endurance of totalitarian conditions but also how the dynamics of (and conservatism within) public services education acts as a brake. This is what is at threat through neoliberal marketisation and neoconservative morality projects, notably the destruction of a 'system' where bureaucratic structures stabilise and provide spaces for political action. I would agree that the post-war education bureaucracy needed reform; Ranson (2000: 266) encapsulates how 'democracy has been at a distance from the communities it was created to serve'. However, the path that has been followed has not been one of democratic renewal but a series of regulation and deregulation projects underpinned by a hodgepodge of ideas and beliefs legitimised by functional research and normative exhortations to lead and be led.

The catastrophe in public services education in England is therefore located within the politics of knowledge production, or rather the disappearance of politics by an alliance of elite consumerism and private beliefs. This thinking with Arendt has enabled the relationship between the state, public policy and knowledge to be engaged with in ways that show how the official canon of codified good practice denies the active dialogue within the plurality of theories, methodologies and methods; and, how through colonised professional practice and commissioned research projects people have learned to labour and potentially work, but not to take action. Arendt asks humans to think about the relational threads of what 'I' and 'we' are doing: the failure to recognise natality and pluralism, particularly evident in the mediocrity of an over-indulgence in metrics and 'what works' prescriptions. 'I' and 'we' cannot be spontaneous and do new things while 'I' and 'we' are filling in forms and working out how to handle the next inspection visit.

This is beyond the ELMA field and speaks to all those involved in public services, but for now I intend focusing specifically on the dilemmas for this field through examining the issue of gender as a matter of practice and the study of that practice. In doing so I will define the problem and show how Arendt's approach can help the field think itself out of that problem, and I will also show how Arendt is also limited for that thinking. In doing this I would like to demonstrate that the field needs to rethink its approach to consuming, and using seemingly neutral strategies, such as transformational leadership, towards identifying, using and debating the intellectual resources necessary to think about thinking.

The gender agenda

The problem of gender reveals itself within ELMA in two main ways: there is the issue of practice and the composition of the workforce, and there is the study of that practice in the largely gender-blind research projects and training manuals. I am not the first to say this and won't be the last, but here I would like to provide a summary of the situation as a precursor to thinking historically and politically.

A consistent feature of research internationally is that women dominate the profession but a greater proportion of male teachers are in leadership positions (Coleman 2002, McNamara *et al.* 2008, 2010, Ribbins 2008). Research by Howson (2007, 2008) and Sprigade and Howson (2011) in England shows that women are breaking through into leadership roles, particularly in primary and special schools, but it remains the case that they are under-represented:

> Although women take the majority of posts in the primary sector, they are still under-represented in appointments to senior posts compared with their overall percentage of the profession, mostly markedly in the secondary sector where an oft observed 'glass ceiling' at around 40% of appointments still seems to be firmly in place.
>
> (Sprigade and Howson 2001: unpaged, Issues Section)

Research continues to show discrimination and gendered organisational cultures that impact on how educational professionals engage in professional practice and think about promotion (e.g. Courtney 2011, McNamara *et al.* 2009). McNamara *et al.* (2010) show that research into the gendered division of labour can position women as deficit, particularly through biological accounts and analyses of organisational barriers where women are deemed to be the problem. More productive accounts focus on how gendered power relations can be identified through the realities of professional practice, and the need for inter-sectionality with class, race, ethnicity, sexuality and race. However, what remains problematic is how research is designed, conducted and funded:

> The child who said, 'Yikes! That emperor has no clothes!' was like the young scholars today who are researching the issue of women in school leadership. The methodological and theoretical leaps of the past three decades lend support to those who actively research questions that challenge the emperor. The repressed truths about persistent under-representation of women in educational management positions and the ways the scholars, the knowledge base, the professional culture have perpetuated this repression, are a naked embarrassment. Though the child and scholars may be shushed for challenging hegemony, they know what they see.
>
> (Marshall 2000: 699)

Within the field in England there is the case that researchers are 'shushed' but more disturbingly contemporary history shows that researchers have been complicit in the 'repression'.

The conceptualisation of field purposes and practices in England has a history of gender blindness, and this is politically located in the male domination of the field and the characterisation of activity separate from the unjust world in which the people who may engage in that activity actually live and practise. The main debates seem to be about the 'applied' nature of the field and the utility of the social sciences in organisational problem solving, rather than critical analyses of the sourcing and application of masculine knowledge production as a form of oppression for professionals and children. So major texts that can be regarded as milestones in knowledge production over time either tend not to include considerations of gender (e.g. Baron and Taylor 1969, Hughes *et al.* 1985) or take an 'and gender' approach where a section or chapter is slotted in but the main gender-neutral theories and research remain intact (e.g. Bush 2011, Coleman and Earley 2005, Law and Glover 2000). Texts directly linked to the development of professional capabilities over a number of decades also fail to engage with this (e.g. Busher and Harris 2000, Davies *et al.* 1990, Davies 2005, Everard and Morris 1988, Harris and Bennett 2001, Hargreaves and Hopkins 1991, Hopkins 2001, 2007, John 1980, Knight 1989, Marland 1986); book series linked to postgraduate programmes show this (Bush 1989, Glatter 1989, Levacic 1989, Preedy *et al.* 2003), or have an 'and gender' (or 'and diversity') approach (e.g. Bennett *et al.* 1992, Bennett et al. 2003a, Bush and Bell 2002, Crawford *et al.* 1997, Harris *et al.* 1997, Kydd *et al.* 2003, Preedy *et al.* 1997, Preedy *et al.* 2012, Riches and Morgan 1989). While the National College in England has commissioned research on gender (e.g. Coleman 2004) this has not impacted on preferred leadership models offered to the profession.

The dearth of historical work within the field, or even locating active professionals as historically located subjects, means that the professional does not have access to an Arendtian approach to 'a life lived as action that can be narrativised and shared by others who did not necessarily participate in the narrated action' (Tamboukou 2010: 117). So the intellectual resources that professional researchers and researching professionals draw on ensure that real lives cannot be spoken, and injustices are at best tokenised but are usually marginalised, and this made the field accessible for the TLP. Research that examines issues of gender (e.g. Ouston 1993) and women heads (e.g. Coleman 2001, Hall 1996), together with issues of intersectionality (e.g. Courtney 2011), remain out of sight, and no serious rethinking about field purposes and knowledge takes place. It seems as if this type of work is happening internationally (e.g. Blackmore and Sachs 2007), with isolated activity in England (e.g. Lumby and Coleman 2007).

Hall (1999) provides a useful metaphor and explanation of this situation, where she experiences isolation, and how in her positioning within an edited collection she enables the 'and gender' issue to be revealed (Bush *et al.* 1999):

> a cynic might ask why we need yet another paper on gender and educational management when the bookshelves are heavy with them. Yet a look at the bibliography of this chapter compared with the bibliographies of other chapters in the book will demonstrate precisely why yet another paper is necessary, though not whether it will achieve anything by being written. As I try to show, the debate about gender and educational management continues to be carried out mainly by women about women. The few men represented in the bibliography have entered it by talking about men and neither group of authors is likely to have made it into the other bibliographies contained in this volume ... Only when volumes like this do not have a separate chapter on gender or equality and the chapter bibliographies are peppered with references relating to these issues will we know some progress has been made.
>
> (Hall 1999: 155–156)

It seems that Hall (1999) is speaking in ways that have an Arendtian flavour about them: she recognises the need and possibility for something new to happen but the distance between researchers (at separate tables) is too much, and so politics and action are impossible. Hall (1999) argues for challenging assumptions and definitions made about and within knowledge production:

> the time is ripe for a new taken-for-grantedness in defining, researching and practicing educational management – one that includes how organisations reproduce and reinforce masculinities and femininities and the consequence of this for the educational experiences and opportunities of those the organisation are there to serve: the learners, whether children or adults.
>
> (ibid.: 164)

In Arendtian terms it seems that adults may be taking responsibility for children and their learning through the effective and efficient leadership and management of a school, but in doing so they are advantaging a particular group and they are preparing children for the world without giving recognition to the realities of lived lives. Over 15 years since this chapter was published, and even though there have been teachable moments provoked through data and events, the situation is not much different. The popularising of emotional intelligence where leaders have to engage in so called 'soft' feminine type behaviours such as listening is a co-option of gender by the TLP rather than a resolution of gender injustices. So the question that I want to ask is: how might Arendt's approach to thinking politically and historically help provoke the field into action? I intend to do this by drawing on debates about Arendt's ideas on the 'social', and the 'boomerang thesis'.

Thinking with the social

Arendt's own achievements combined with her recognition of women's lives (e.g. Arendt 1993, 1994) suggests that she could be a role model for the feminist movement. However, it seems that her distinctions between labour, work and action condemn traditional women's work to low-status labour. As such Arendt has been labelled as an example of 'female male-supremacists' (O'Brien 1981: 9) and *The Human Condition* as a 'lofty and crippled book' (Rich 1979: 211–212). However, Honig (1995) recognises that shifts in feminist thinking enables Arendt's utility to come to the fore, particularly through the rejection of binaries (e.g. masculine, feminine) in favour of political action:

> The 'Arendt Question in Feminism' pushes feminists into an engagement with Arendt that is not merely a reinterrogation of her work but a dynamic and mutual encounter. While those who posed the 'Woman Question in Arendt' thought Arendt's public/private distinction was obviously and hopelessly masculinist, feminists who pose the 'Arendt Question in Feminism' are prodded to reconsider their own commitment to dismantle that distinction. The question is no longer simply, How does feminist theory change the way we think about Arendt? but also always, How does reading Arendt change the way we think about feminist theory?
>
> (Honig 1995: 3)

So I could appropriate this question as follows: how does reading Arendt change the way the field thinks about theory?

Addressing this question can be started through Pitkin's (1998) engagement with Arendt's conceptualisation of the social in *The Human Condition* through adopting a cultural metaphor drawn from the film *The Attack of the Blob*:

> It's like a science-fiction fantasy: Arendt writes about the social as if an evil monster from outer space, entirely external to and separate from us, had fallen upon us intent on debilitating, absorbing, and

ultimately destroying us, gobbling up our distinct individuality and
turning us into robots that mechanically serve its purposes.

(Pitkin 1998: 4)

What Arendt is talking about is how the person takes action, engages in
politics and experiences freedom. For Arendt, the emphasis on the social
rather than the political has created a trap of ordinariness that breeds
conformity and legitimises the prevalence of labour. Owens (2011: 16)
builds on this analysis and argues that it is the drive for security which is
blob-like:

> To modify Pitkin's analysis of Arendt's writing on the social, security
> and so-called processes of 'securitisation' have absorbed, embraced and
> devoured people or other entities, such as the environment, health,
> citizenship, finance, and religion; security has emerged, grown, and let
> loose the growth of bureaucracy, surveillance and other forms of
> administrative control; it has entered, intruded on, and conquered
> the once separate and discrete realms of war, politics and strategy; it
> has constituted and controlled populations, transformed and even
> perverted the political realm; those in apparent possession of security
> expertise have imposed rules on people, demanded certain forms of
> conduct from them, excluded or refused to admit other conduct or
> people. Far more than Arendt's concept of the social, security is like a
> gigantic and devouring globule of jelly; we are and have for some time
> been undergoing an attack of the security Blob.

This Blob is all-consuming, where the self and organisational discipline
brings security through audits and performance regimes; and security
through regulation is evident in the risk management ways of thinking
and tick the box reflexes. It seems to me that managerialism (as distinct
from management) is Blob-like in how new power relations and processes
construct security in ways that make the worker actually feel insecure. As
Wacquant (2009) has argued, while the economy has been deregulated
with risk taking as a cultural trope for success, in all other activity there
must be the regulation of risk through the creation of fear. The population
needs to be socially controlled through neoliberal and neoconservative
security measures: notably with a shift from welfare, to workfare, to
prisonfare:

> neoliberal penality does coalesce around the shrill reassertion of penal
> fortitude, the pornographic exhibition of the taming of moral and
> criminal deviancy, and the punitive containment and disciplinary

supervision of the problem populations dwelling at the margins of the class and cultural order. Bringing developments on the social welfare and crime control fronts into a single analytic frame reveals that, for the precarious fractions of the urban proletariat that are their privileged clientele, the programmatic convergence and practical interlock of restrictive 'workfare' and expansive 'prisonfare' gives the neoliberal state a distinctively parternalistic visage and translates into intensified intrusion and castigatory oversight.

(Wacquant 2009: xx–xxi)

The social requires security, and security requires control processes: while managerialist processes seem logical, change to working lives and practices has not happened rationally or in a carefully planned way, but is about pursuing capital accumulation through pragmatic strategising. So as Hind (2010: 20) argues, hope of rewards operates in ways that can seem liberating, so 'the powerless compete to tell the powerful what they want to hear, while the powerful move to suppress the civic virtues that would threaten their control of the state'.

ELMA has been consumed by the neoliberal and neoconservative TLP security-driven social Blob, and ELMA has become a benign title for how the Blob consumes educational professionals through the functionality of technical processes and exhortations to do better. So gender (and other structural injustice issues) as a matter of research and practice remain an unresolved issue for and within the field because of narrow research conceptualisations and limited scholarship. Managerialism only produces a particular type of data, whereas dealing with social injustice requires a range of data – both statistical and experiential. My own research into the growth of ELMA shows that field members have collaborated with the data collection required by neoliberal and neoconservative projects, and so it seems that what matters is what is funded (Gunter 2012a). Arendt's thinking and debates about that thinking enables the professional practice of an epistemic group (and associated groups) to be understood as fabricators of freedom. While the language and message of globalised texts has been about self-management and strategy (e.g. Caldwell and Spinks 1988) and collaboration and support (Hopkins 2007), in reality there is no freedom in Barber's (2007) policy deliverology or in New Labour's earned autonomy through compliance with demands for the right type of data. Arendt's analysis enables the depoliticisation of education to be given recognition: policy, it seems, determines the need for effective and efficient ELMA rather than creates opportunities for political debate and action; and, as such, ELMA largely fails to engage with the theories located within the plurality of the knowledge, knowing and knowers within the field of study and practice.

Thinking with the 'boomerang thesis'

In *On Totalitarianism* Arendt (2009) presents an analysis of what she calls the 'real and immediate boomerang effects' (p206) in regard to the relationship between conduct in colonial life and back in the home nation:

> This European experience in the colonies, which was fed by and bred a psychology of domination, had far-reaching effects back in Europe. Racist theories and non-democratic political assumptions (rule by decree and enforcement by bureaucracy) and particular practices (forced population transfers, protogenocidal massacres, and a profound heedlessness about human life) fed back into European (and Western hemispheric) political and intellectual cultures. For instance, colonial powers tested the early use of aerial bombardment upon subject populations in their colonies, while Hitler was a great admirer of the British Empire, and Nazi Germany formulated its racial laws of 1935 using the example of the South in the United States. The result was a strengthening of authoritarian modes of political rule, along with something approaching an addiction to racial thinking and augmentation of racist ideologies in Europe, particularly after the early 1880s. Moreover, the ideology of imperial grandeur and/or mission helped mask class and ideological fissures in various European societies.
>
> (King and Stone 2008: 2–3)

For Arendt (2009: 221) 'the stage seemed to be set for all possible horrors', but some caveats regarding her thesis need to be made. Following King and Stone (2008) it is important to recognise that first, colonialism and imperialism were not the only causes of totalitarianism; second, the relationship between imperialism and racism was not just an issue for Germany but also across Europe; and third, while the boomerang thesis is 'brilliantly provocative . . . it is seriously underdeveloped . . . [and so] . . . it is best considered, we would suggest, as a research hypothesis rather than a fully proven historical claim' (King and Stone 2008: 3). With this in mind I intend thinking about ELMA using the boomerang hypothesis to think about how ELMA gendered ideas travel and impact globally through the TLP.

Education policies do travel the world, and notably neoliberal and conservative projects have generated systemic reforms and restructuring combined with cultural changes and normalised discourses. Specifically charter schools in the US and free schools in Sweden have given governments in England the confirmation of the reality of schools outside of local democratic control. In addition there is imperialism where the opening of local markets to global investment and profit making makes education systems subject to invasion, with the potentional of for-profit companies taking over schools in England (Gunter 2011). England has been and continues to be an initiative laboratory for the privatisation of schooling, where proponents have travelled with their ideas (e.g. Barber 2007), and researchers have identified the way this operates in a post-colonial context (e.g. Berkhout 2007, Fitzgerald 2007).

The field of ELMA has a historical dependency on global networks, particularly links within the Commonwealth (e.g. Gunter 1999), and so field members have been active in travelling the world in seeking out and promoting new models. A good example of this is the model of good leadership practice known as transformational leadership, whereby the emphasis is on eradicating natality and spontaneity through the affective relationship between leader and follower. The attractiveness of transformational leadership is that it is presented as neutral and so can travel, but it is a product of the capitalist means of production that is consistent with hierarchical cultures within western-style democracies. Notably this is what Blackmore (1999) means when in concluding her analysis of 'troubling women' she not only shows how women are excluded and so are trouble, but she makes the point that 'perhaps the focus upon leadership is itself the biggest barrier to gender equality' (p222). For a model that has been presented as enabling practice to improve, it has generated a culture where both men and women have not sought promotion in sufficient numbers. Interestingly this has been used to show the deficits within professional cultures, and how educational services need to be delivered by those who have learned to labour outside of education.

As already noted, ELMA has translated activism into accepting (or possibly reworking) neoliberal/neoconservative projects as being 'in the interests of children' where localised modification is about protecting children, combined with a pragmatic approach to how the reform can be used to deal with local problems (e.g. a difficult member of staff, a department that needs to improve). I want to use an example of workforce remodelling in England as an example of a gender-neutral transformational leadership project that was redeveloped as a result of the 1988 Education Reform Act and brought about site-based management and business processes regarding the composition of the workforce (Butt and Gunter 2007). When New Labour took office in 1997 they dealt with the staffing crisis (not enough people going into or staying in teaching) through a remodelling project where they put emphasis on non-teachers in taking on aspects of teachers' work, particularly the role of teaching assistants within the classroom and in 'covering' lessons when a teacher is absent. The growth of non-QTS assistants doing teaching has been a key feature of the project, as well as an increased emphasis on leaders from outside of the teaching profession leading educational services (see DfES/PwC 2007). This deregulation of the profession continues where the investment in free schools has enabled professional practice to be opened up to non-qualified 'teachers'. On one level the issue is whether children need to be taught at all or can learn by themselves, or whether they need to be taught by adults who have undergone a period of advanced education, such as a degree, and who have specific training in teaching and learning. Underlying this is whether all children have an entitlement to an education, or whether basic literacies plus work-related training is sufficient. I would like to illuminate this by raising the issue of 'hole in the wall' computers as a potential boomerang policy.

Judge (2000) has reported on the educational experiments conducted by Sugata Mitra, who has used 'hole in the wall' computers as a means of helping India's poorest children:

> He believes that children, even terribly poor kids with little education, can quickly teach themselves the rudiments of computer literacy. The key, he contends, is for teachers and other adults to give them free rein, so their natural curiosity takes over and they teach themselves. He calls the concept 'minimally invasive education.'
>
> To test his ideas, Mitra 13 months ago launched something he calls 'the hole in the wall experiment.' He took a PC connected to a high-speed data connection and imbedded it in a concrete wall next to NIIT's headquarters in the south end of New Delhi. The wall separates the company's grounds from a garbage-strewn empty lot used by the poor as a public bathroom. Mitra simply left the computer on, connected to the Internet, and allowed any passerby to play with it. He monitored activity on the PC using a remote computer and a video camera mounted in a nearby tree.
>
> What he discovered was that the most avid users of the machine were ghetto kids aged 6 to 12, most of whom have only the most rudimentary education and little knowledge of English. Yet within days, the kids had taught themselves to draw on the computer and to browse the Net. Some of the other things they learned, Mitra says, astonished him.
>
> The physicist has since installed a computer in a rural neighborhood with similar results. He's convinced that 500 million children could achieve basic computer literacy over the next five years, if the Indian government put 100,000 Net-connected PCs in schools and trained teachers in some basic 'noninvasive' teaching techniques for guiding children in using them.
>
> (Judge 2000: unpaged)

There are important issues about the globalisation of privatisation that come from this intervention (see Ball 2012). Some are about integrity in the sense that children and their community are being experimented on without consent, and without a robust methodology and method. Some are educational, through how the children learn about the use of machinery and software, but beyond that it seems that getting the right answers rather than understanding what they know and how they know it is what matters. Teachers would recognise the ingenuity of students to investigate and learn, but would also know about the importance of pedagogic interventions to lift the acquisition of techniques for learning through knowledge about how children learn, how children talk and how children in groups work together. Significantly it seems that the approach is about business, where children need to be computer literate in order to operate in the market place: they need to know how to buy online and they need to be accessed by online advertisers. That Judge (2000) reports on the lack of equity issues is also important: it seems that women adults who do not access the computer don't matter as the focus is on the next generation.

Arendt's analysis generates questions about how the English context is receptive to this type of 'educational' innovation. Poverty in England as an affluent society is an issue that is not easy to resolve (see Raffo *et al.* 2010), where questions and answers travel internationally, and the use of ICT as a solution to those issues is one that has been used both in England (Butt and Gunter 2007) and clearly in India as a post-colonial society. If poor children in India can gain access to learning without trained and publicly funded teachers and schools then the remodelling and privatising agenda in England could be further enhanced by the 'hole in the wall' experiment. Indeed, if as reported, 54 million days of school were missed last year through children truanting from school in England (Richardson 2012), then a 'hole in the wall' computer might just solve the problem. Neoliberals could argue that as consumers their needs are not being met, and neoconservatives would panic over so many children on the streets, an issue that they are increasingly resolving through home schooling and controlling local schooling through free schools.

It seems that the problem of poor children in England could be dealt with through access to residual basic functional skills needed to operate in the labour and consumer market place, and so remove the burden from the taxpayer for schools, teachers and a wider curriculum. Such an argument has been framed productively as 'personalisation', and it speaks to the deprofessionalisation discourse in England by generating rhetorical claims that standards can be secured without trained teachers. Indeed, another potential 'boomerang' policy is how the functionality of teacher training in

England could be made more efficient (and cost effective) by adopting the approach developed by Stanford University and Pearson in the US. Instead of a student teacher being watched in the classroom with a follow on professional conversation, two ten-minute vidoes are recorded of them teaching and then sent for scoring by independent assessors. Winerip (2012) reports on resistance to this, but this case illustrates how the dominant discourse is that entrepreneurs know best, and espouse a remit that is about a business case that trumps an educational, or professional, or citizenship one. As Ball (2012) shows, experiments with vouchers, choice processes and for profit education for the poor are being developed by neoliberal consultants in different parts of the world, and may colonise and/or re-colonise England.

Research shows that headteachers can and do position themselves differently: some have accepted the implementation mode while others are ambivalent and worry, and others fire back with localised policy developments (Gunter and Forrester 2009). The complexity of the realities of policy processes within schools, particularly since some are under surveillance more than others, means that implementation is messy. However, the barrier to the boomerang effects of experiments such as the 'hole in the wall' is that it is seemingly a good idea, and arguing against any initiative that gives children *any* opportunities to learn *something* is really difficult. In addition, the impact of over 30 years of neoliberal projects for the workforce and children does mean that activity is increasingly disconnected from values: professionals do things that they do not necessarily believe in and so end up being ventriloquists for powerful voices.

What is happening to publicly funded education in England is brutal, as millions of children are being deemed superfluous to investment in democratic citizenship and thousands of professionals are being disappeared. What does this mean for ELMA? The challenge is to directly and critically engage with the mediocrity of the TLP by working with the profession in developing alternatives. An appropriate starting point is structural and cultural disadvantage, and I have focused on gender and interplayed it with poverty, but there are other important matters such as class, race, age and sexuality, which ELMA has failed to systematically engage with. So there is a political research imperative for field members and a political literacy imperative for professional 'pre' and 'in' service programmes. Arendt's analysis of the *vita activa* and the *vita contemplativa* is helpful because it inspires and enables the type of political action that is needed to question knowledge production within the field. For example, scrutinising the knowledge base of the field enables basic questions to be asked about the failure to look south in order to examine reform programmes (Apple 2005) and theories (Connell 2007).

In making these arguments I am mindful about how shocking this analysis can be and how negative reactions might be used against the development of scholarly and professional practice. Indeed, King and Stone (2008) note the challenges generated by the 'boomerang thesis', where they sum up the arguments that: first, the causes of totalitarianism in Germany are located more in the post-World War One conditions than in the German imperial experience, and so it could be argued that the situation in public education in England is more a product of professional failure than of the export and import of neoliberal/neoconservative solutions; second, in some countries colonial conduct was the same or worse than in Germany but a totalitarian regime did not develop, and so it could be argued that innovations from abroad need not damage public education; and third, debates have taken place about how Arendt characterised sub-Saharan Africans as 'uncivilised' (King and Stone 2008: 11) and as such she has been seen as Euro-centric or indeed racist, and so it could be argued that failing to learn as a researcher is a colonial legacy. These are serious matters, and can suggest that how a situation is read, understood and acted upon matters the most.

What I would like to contribute through the analysis so far in reply to these points is: first, research shows that the relationship between the teaching profession and the state has been difficult (Moran 2007), but it is clear that reform has been mainly through neoliberal projects designed to make publicly funded teachers realistically recultured as deliverers of other people's plans, and so potentially superfluous; second, Arendtian analysts are clear that totalitarian conditions do not necessarily lead to totalitarianism, and so I have been mindful to acknowledge that the crystallisation process is not inevitable or rational, but the questions that need to be asked are about the positions and roles that ELMA field members are taking; and, third, the limitations of research and researchers in how issues are problematised and engaged with is something that I am mindful of and certainly ELMA needs to embrace different arguments about knowledge production. However, what is of interest is how interventions are made into children's lives in ways that must be questioned – no matter where they come from, particularly how damage can be done through importing models such as transformational leadership and education for profit provision. My support for the arguments that there is a need to learn from the south is not to accept that the solution to poverty and the provision of educational services lies there or to displace other sites of learning. Rather, Arendt's arguments about pluralism and the opportunities located within natality generate thinking that can enable ELMA to think and act in ways that are more than implementation and delivery.

A final point is about the relationship between education and politics. This is not just a policy issue but one that is inherently pedagogic. As a reminder, in the essays 'The crisis in education' and 'Little Rock' Arendt argues that children should not be used to work out political problems that adults should take responsibility for, and through this children should not be reproducing structural injustices because of a deficit location in power relations. Part of my objection to the 'hole in the wall' experiments is that children are coerced into justifying adult plans, and responsibility for research requires a robust design and integrity. However, I need to address Arendt's claim that education and politics should be separate, and in engaging with this Levinson (2001: 30) argues: 'Arendt is not attempting to separate politics and education into distinct spheres. She is, rather, attempting to distinguish the kinds of responsibilities and qualities demanded of us when we teach from those required of us in politics.'

In summary, any engagement with education means that adults take responsibility for and within the gap between past and present, so that students can understand their positioning and the possibilities for something new. It seems to me that this is a place the TLP does not go to. Children are simultaneously the reason to be in the job, to work on their behalf, but children are positioned as objects upon which these elite adults impact. The failure of ELMA to engage with pedagogy, except as an organisational process to be led and managed, means that the responsibility of the teacher in addition to targets and outcomes is not being thought through. Indeed, Duarte (2010b: 263) argues that 'teachers must let-go of their own desire for specific outcomes, especially those that are identified as "political" outcomes'. Delivering government reforms is a political outcome, and what needs to be focused on is thinking, which Duarte (2009: 250) argues 'requires the teacher to sublimate her desire for confirmation of her own knowledge'. So issues such as gender and poverty need to be addressed through the pedagogic process:

> The 'crisis' in social justice education is the ever present turning point when the educator chooses to let a student's thinking be free and independent of her own projects. In making this choice, and projecting the clearing for the time and place of thinking, the educator takes a leap of faith in the student's capacity to think differently, and thereby chooses to *be* the very justice she wants to see in the world.
>
> (Duarte 2009: 252)

This matter cannot be resolved here; suffice to say that Arendt's approach to political action, pluralism and freedom can enable ELMA to think productively about teaching and learning as a non-TLP project. ELMA members need to think themselves out of confirming the knowledge and ways of knowing that are given to them to tweak, apply and update; ELMA members need a justice agenda for their own development and the processes that they use to take action. In doing this ELMA members need to look, read and discuss beyond the Arendtian library, not least because between the period of neglect and the current revival in interest in her work there have been important theoretical and methodological developments that are a resource and could challenge in different ways. Perhaps the relationship between ideas and action, where I started in Chapter 1, is a productive place for vital intellectual work to take place.

A pause

The book series in which this particular text is located is about enabling ELMA to develop a sense of itself regarding the purposes and practices of knowledge production. The characterisation of the leadership turn in the field, as related to and constructed by the TLP, enables field members to interrogate the conduct and meaning of professional practice. Each of the texts in the series takes a different but interrelated position on this matter, and through thinking politically and historically with Arendt's writings I have sought not only to enable ELMA to develop understandings and explanations for the predicaments it now finds itself in, but also to recognise the necessity and means of historical analysis and political action. For Strong (2012) thinking and responsibility are interlinked, whereby we cannot be content that we have a solution because 'responsibility is first and foremost the ability not to do what is wrong, an ability, Arendt indicates, that will be seriously corroded if we try to do what we think it right' (p339). So while historical thinking enables collective memories to be used and protected as a resource, the use of political thinking generates analysis of a dangerous situation: totalitarian conditions remain, TLP good practice is enabling those conditions to crystallise, and TLP labour and work is ensuring that ELMA members are motivated about creating the catastrophe they are located within.

An important starting point could be to focus on knowledge claims and the relationship with methodologies and methods. As a reminder of Arendt's position:

> Arendt had a generally low opinion of the post-war sociological mindset, the chief defect of which she believed was a congenital blindness towards the unique and the unprecedented – whether this was the unpredictable novelty of human action, or the radically new regime, which in the case of Nazism seemed to mark a decisive break with the whole philosophical and political tradition of the West, that was

totalitarianism. The banal generalisations of the positivist sociologist had too much in common, from Arendt's viewpoint, with the banality of thought characteristic of the bureaucrat. Both served to normalise the unprecedented and the unacceptable, while their fetishising of disinterestedness . . . ignored the 'methodological necessity' of bearing testimony to the appalling nature of dehumanising conditions, no matter how routinised or familiar.

(Bowring 2011: 231)

It seems to me that there are many in ELMA who would agree that much social science research is too abstract and self-reverential, and indeed Greenfield's challenge to the field in 1974 is very much located in a concern to recognise realism and values (Greenfield and Ribbins 1993). However, what thinking with Arendt does is to question the ELMA current obsession with relevance and functionality – as if all situations are the same in place and time – and that having accepted close to practice theorising, in reality the intellectual work being done is not close at all and is not actually educational. It seems that in rejecting supposed 'disinterestedness' by engaging directly with people and professional practices, the field has been open to the TLP that has limited that engagement to popularising leadership products and making 'dehumanising conditions' bearable for most and advantageous for a few.

I would therefore like to leave the field with two main questions to stimulate political thinking and action: first, what are the implications for the professional researcher and researching professional? Arendt is helpful here regarding positioning:

Imagination alone enables us to see things in their proper perspective, to be strong enough to put that which is too close at a certain distance so that we can see and understand it without bias or prejudice, to be generous enough to bridge abysses of remoteness until we can see and understand everything that is too far away from us as though it were our own affair. This distancing of some things and bridging the abysses to others is part of the dialogue of understanding, for whose purposes direct experience establishes too close a contact and mere knowledge erects artificial barriers.

(Arendt 1994: 323)

There are resources to help the field to engage in this historical and political reflexivity, and so Anyon and her colleagues (2009) ensure that the social sciences do not 'have an hypnotic effect' (Arendt 1970: 8) through making explicit the relationship between data, ideas and action: 'the

importance of thinking through how we think *with* theory, as we undertake the analytical labours of research and writing' (Anyon 2009: 7).

The second question is: what are the implications for how research is
read and used? Again Arendt is helpful here:

> Each time you write something and you send it out into the world and
> it becomes public, obviously everybody is free to do with it what he
> pleases, and this is as it should be. I do not have any quarrel with this.
> You should not try to hold your hand now on whatever may happen to
> what you have been thinking for yourself. You should rather try to
> learn from what other people do with it.
>
> (Arendt 1973, cited in Canovan 1998: xx)

Focusing on the type and quality of debates in research outputs, reviews
and at conferences is a productive means through which researchers can
seek to learn what happens when ideas are listened to or read or even
ignored. Again there are historical resources in the field to help us to do
this; Greenfield's (1978, Greenfield and Ribbins 1993) experiences show
how difficult it is to demonstrate pluralism, and what he learned about
what other people did with it:

> I have watched with surprise and fascination the furore which began
> with the presentation of my paper at the IIP in 1974. A Thursday, I
> think it was, in Bristol. People ask me if the reaction bothers me. No
> it doesn't. The slings and arrows of academic warfare are not unpleasant.
> Somewhat like St. Sebastian, I suppose, I'd rather be in pain as long as
> the crowd understands what the ceremony is about. But it is hard just
> to be written off, ignored or buried.
>
> (Greenfield 1978: 86–87)

Greenfield (1978) argues that his lack of an invitation to the 1978
International Intervisitation Programme (IIP) is connected to the inability
of the field to engage in robust debate about theory, and while there is a
genuine desire to talk they do not want to be involved in 'an unfortunate
battle in rather poor taste which somehow demeans theory and the past
glory of the field of study' (p83). He shows exasperation in being unable to
get his colleagues to ask different questions, and four years on from the
1974 IIP he reveals that what he said was not new but it was to him and
to his audience, and 'the real value then of the IIP paper and of the symposium may be the debate itself' (p98). Not all of our debates need to be a
form of combat, but we do need to examine such challenges to knowledge
claims and how they are received, used and engaged with.

So I pause at this point and remind the reader that what thinking with Arendt has done is to make explicit that the unthinkable is happening – schools are being taken away from children, families and communities. Discuss.

We live in, to paraphrase Arendt, dark times, and so the strategy is one of illumination and how the ELMA field takes action. Professionals have withdrawn into getting on with the job or into retirement, and researchers have withdrawn, as Tamboukou (2012) argues, into the library, and in doing so the world is damaged. As Apple (2010) reminds us, in higher education we have privileges and responsibilities that need to be deployed carefully in relation to our students and communities. We remain well versed in the limitations of the field, but as Niesche (2012) states, there is within the world research that does a different type of job than that designed and generated by the TLP gurus. So the issue is how we might rethink our position and rescript our place in higher education:

> although fearless speech is open to everyone, academics as teachers and pedagogues have assumed extra responsibilities in sustaining the web of human relations and opening up potential sites where students can be educated in telling the truth as they see it, but also in listening to others.
>
> (Tamboukou 2012: 13)

Think, talk and decide what you, along with others, are going to do about the unfolding catastrophe in education.

Annotated bibliography

Introduction

The readings I am presenting here are ones that enable either the first-time reader to begin to engage with Arendt's writings and/or the reader already familiar with Arendt to develop understandings of her work on education. In doing so I am presenting this as a rational account with lists of texts in clear sections, but there is nothing more exciting than just diving in and enjoying the intellectual swim through the challenge of ideas and thinking. My advice is to think about an issue that is currently on your mind, and in thinking it through you could do no better than to follow Arendt's advice:

> Like a pearl diver who descends to the bottom of the sea, not to excavate the bottom and bring it to light but to pry loose the rich and the strange, the pearls and the coral in the depths and to carry them to the surface, this thinking delves into the depths of the past – but not in order to resuscitate it the way it was and to contribute to the renewal of extinct ages. What guides this thinking is the conviction that although the living is subject to the ruin of time, the process of decay is at the same time a process of crystallization, that in the depth of the sea, into which sinks and is dissolved what once was alive, some things 'suffer a sea-change' and survive in new crystallized forms and shapes that remain immune to the elements, as though they waited only for the pearl diver who one day will come down to them and bring them up into the world of the living – as 'thought fragments', as something 'rich and strange', and perhaps even as everlasting *Urphänomene*.
>
> (Arendt 1993: 205–206, emphasis in original)

Saying this is easier than doing it, but it is in the doing that enables the relationship between ideas and action to be opened up to reflexive processes and scrutiny. I am attracted to, and I use, metaphors to bring perspectives to this process, and so I find 'pearl divers', along with others used in this book such as 'banisters', to be provoking and enabling. This is not an original thought, as others who have been there before me have noted the productive challenges involved:

Thinking is a mode of constantly questioning the meaning that one wishes to attribute to some aspect of the world. Such questioning is not designed to arrive at a final conclusion and give itself peace. Rather, it is to question constantly, including oneself. It is, thus, a form of responsibility, of not claiming that which cannot be claimed, namely, that one can and has come to a conclusion about how the world is. (There is an insight here into Socrates' claim that all that he knew is that he knew nothing.) And, as a form of responsibility, thinking is, thus, clearly a necessary precondition for political being-in-the-world. Responsibility is first and foremost the ability not to do what is wrong, an ability, Arendt indicates, that will be seriously corroded if we try to do what we think is right.

(Strong 2012: 339)

So for those who do and research leaders, leading and leadership in educational organisations and processes there is a requirement to read and think responsibly.

Works of Hannah Arendt

My recommendation is that the reader engages with the following works (these editions are the ones that I have used):

Arendt, H. (1958) *The Human Condition*. Second edition. Chicago: The University of Chicago Press.
Arendt, H. (1963) *Eichmann in Jerusalem*. London: Penguin Books.
Arendt, H. (1970) *On Violence*. Orlando, FL: A Harvest Book, Harcourt Inc.
Arendt, H. (1972) *Crises of the Republic*. New York, NY: Harcourt Brace Jovanovich Inc.
Arendt, H. (1978) *The Life of the Mind*. New York, NY: Harcourt Inc.
Arendt, H. (1993) *Men in Dark Times*. San Diego: A Harvest Book, Harcourt Brace & Company.
Arendt, H. (1994) *Essays in Understanding, 1930–1954: Formation, Exile and Totalitarianism*. New York, NY: Schocken Books.
Arendt, H. (2003) *Responsibility and Judgement*. New York, NY: Schocken Books.
Arendt, H. (2006a) *Between Past and Future*. New York, NY: Penguin Books.
Arendt, H. (2006b) *On Revolution*. New York, NY: Penguin Books.
Arendt, H. (2009) *The Origins of Totalitarianism* (1958, second edition). Garsington: Benediction Books.

While diving in is a sensible piece of advice – that is what I did – it could well be that personal preferences may need some recommendations. As I show in this book there is the view that the best starting point is *The Origins of Totalitarianism*, and I agree with that. This is the site of important political and historical analysis, and the debates about this text (see below) are most enriching. Readers who find grand sweeps of history together with evidential stories and analysis should also look at Arendt (2006a, 2006b). However, readers may find Arendt's works regarding humanity more congenial and so two good starting points would be

The Human Condition and *The Life of the Mind*. Others may find the focus on events and people a more attractive starting point, and so the account of the Eichman trial or *Men in Dark Times* are good places to consider the interplay between the agency of humanity and the structuring impact of context and ideas.

Readers may decide to delve deeper into Arendt's outputs, in which case a really good list is included at the end of Young-Bruehl (1982). In addition to this there are archives of her papers that are of interest, and my recommendation is that the reader engages with the following links:

http://www.bard.edu/arendtcollection/
http://memory.loc.gov/ammem/arendthtml/arendthome.html

These archival collections not only conserve Arendt's own library and documentation but are also in the process of being digitised as a means of opening up access for scholars.

Secondary sources

Beginning to map and to develop a historiography of the field of Arendtian studies for this book has led me to recognise that there are a number of texts that serve a range of purposes.

I would recommend the following texts that cover Arendt's life and work, and the relationship between the two:

Baehr, P. (2003) Editor's introduction. In: Baehr, P. (ed.) *The Portable Hannah Arendt*. London: Penguin Books: vii–liv.
Benhabib, S. (2000) *The Reluctant Modernism of Hannah Arendt*. Lanham, MD: Rowman and Littlefield Publishers Inc.
Bowring, F. (2011) *Hannah Arendt: A Critical Introduction*. London: Pluto Press.
Canovan, M. (1995) *Hannah Arendt: A Reinterpretation of Her Political Thought*. Cambridge: Cambridge University Press.
Watson, D. (1992) *Arendt*. London: Fontana Press.
Young-Bruehl, E. (1982) *Hannah Arendt: For Love of the World*. New Haven: Yale University Press.
Young-Bruehl, E. (2006) *Why Arendt Matters*. New Haven: Yale University Press.

I would recommend the following texts that examine the politics within and of Arendt's thinking and claims:

Brown, D., Bygrave, S. and Morton, S. (2011) Hannah Arendt 'After Modernity'. *New Formations*, Number 71, Spring 2011: 1–139.
Calhoun, C. and McGowan, J. (eds) (1997) *Hannah Arendt and the Meaning of Politics*. Minneapolis, MN: University of Minnesota.
Fraser, N. (2004) Hannah Arendt in the 21st century. *Contemporary Political Theory* 3 (3), 253–261.

126 Annotated bibliography

Honig, B. (ed.) (1995) *Feminist Interpretations of Hannah Arendt*. University Park, PA: Pennsylvania State University Press.

King, R.H. and Stone, D. (2007) (eds) *Hannah Arendt and the Uses of History: Imperialism, Nation, Race, and Genocide*. New York: Berghahn Books: 87–105.

Pitkin, H.F. (1998) *The Attack of the Blob: Hannah Arendt's Concept of the Social*. Chicago, IL: The University of Chicago Press.

Strong, T. (2012) *Politics Without Vision: Thinking Without a Banister in the Twentieth Century*. Chicago, IL: The University of Chicago Press.

Hannah Arendt and education

Primary sources

As I have already noted, Arendt has two main essays that focus on educational issues. The essay on 'Crisis in education' is in *Between Past and Future* (Arendt 2006a); and the essay 'Little Rock' is in *Responsibility and Judgement* (Arendt 2003). These essays need to be read alongside her texts that are not directly focused on education, because her analysis of educational issues speaks to grand challenges about the polity and democratic renewal.

Secondary sources

Educational researchers have found Arendt's work to be good to think with about close to practice issues of teaching and learning, as well as macro issues about the purposes of education.

There are two main collections of papers that I would recommend. The first is the edited collection by Gordon (2001a) where the editor and authors engage with Arendtian thinking as a means of considering the impact that the interruption of her ideas has generated, and to call for more such interruptions. I have found this to be an exciting collection, because at a time of research that is focused on the functionality of what works, these papers give permission to think otherwise and to consider the possibilities of intellectual work. The second is a special issue of *Teachers College Record*, with eight papers plus the editorial introduction (Higgins 2010). The focus is on Arendt's identification of a 'crisis' in education and the interrelationship with *The Human Condition*. The analysis is excellent, and the papers show how Arendt's ideas continue to speak to us 50 years on; the immediate crisis may have passed but the issue of how this relates to educational purposes remains relevant.

In addition to this I have found the growing number of papers from UK educational scholars that are inspired by Arendt (e.g. Samier 2008), focus on methodological issues (e.g. Tamboukou 2010) and use her ideas to think with (e.g. Biesta 2010, Tamboukou 2012) all confirm that Arendt has much to offer. I hope that educational researchers will investigate and use Arendt's methods to think with and to develop important perspectives. In doing so we have the potential to make a contribution to Arendtian studies in ways that are productive and developmental.

References

Anderson, G. (2009) *Advocacy Leadership*. New York: Routledge.

Angus, L. (2012) Teaching within and against the circle of privilege: reforming teachers, reforming schools. *Journal of Education Policy*, 27 (2), 231–251.

Anyon, J. (2009) Introduction. In: Anyon, J. with Dumas, M.J., Linville, D., Nolan, K., Pérez, M., Tuck, E. and Weiss, J., *Theory and Educational Research*. New York, NY: Routledge, 1–23.

Apple, M. W. (2005) Audit cultures, commodification, and class and race strategies in education. *Policy Futures in Education*, 3 (4), 379–399.

Apple, M.W. (ed.) (2010) *Global Crises, Social Justice, and Education*. New York: Routledge.

Apple, M.W. (2011) The politics of compulsory patriotism, on the educational meanings of September 11. In: K.J. Saltman and D.A. Gabbard (eds) *Education as Enforcement*. Second edition. New York, NY: Routledge, 291–300.

Arendt, H. (1958) *The Human Condition*. Second edition. Chicago: The University of Chicago Press.

Arendt, H. (1963) *Eichmann in Jerusalem*. London: Penguin Books.

Arendt, H. (1970) *On Violence*. Orlando, FL: A Harvest Book, Harcourt Inc.

Arendt, H. (1972) *Crises of the Republic*. New York, NY: Harcourt Brace Jovanovich Inc.

Arendt, H. (1978) *The Life of the Mind*. New York, NY: Harcourt Inc.

Arendt, H. (1993) *Men in Dark Times*. San Diego: A Harvest Book, Harcourt Brace & Company.

Arendt, H. (1994) *Essays in Understanding, 1930–1954: Formation, Exile and Totalitarianism*. New York, NY: Schocken Books.

Arendt, H. (2003) *Responsibility and Judgement*. New York, NY: Schocken Books.

Arendt, H. (2005) *The Promise of Politics*. New York, NY: Schocken Books.

Arendt, H. (2006a) *Between Past and Future*. New York, NY: Penguin Books.

Arendt, H. (2006b) *On Revolution*. New York, NY: Penguin Books.

Arendt, H. (2009) *The Origins of Totalitarianism* (1958, second edition). Garsington: Benediction Books.

Arrowsmith, R. (2001) A right performance. In: Gleeson, D. and Husbands, C. (eds) *The Performing School*. London: RoutledgeFalmer, 33–43.

Astle, J. and Ryan, C. (eds) (2008) *Academies and the Future of State Education*. London: CentreForum.

Baehr, P. (2003) Editor's introduction. In: Baehr, P. (ed.) *The Portable Hannah Arendt*. London: Penguin Books, vii–liv.

Ball, S.J. (1990) *Politics and Policymaking in Education*. London: Routledge.

Ball, S.J. (1994) Some reflections on policy theory: a brief response to Hatcher and Troyna. *Journal of Education Policy* 9 (2), 171–182.

Ball, S.J. (1995) Intellectuals or technicians? Urgent role of theory in educational studies. *British Journal of Educational Studies* 43 (3), 255–271.

Ball, S.J. (2003) The teacher's soul and the terrors of performativity. *Journal of Education Policy* 18 (2), 215–228.

Ball, S.J. (2007) *Education PLC*. London: Routledge.

Ball, S.J. (2008) New philanthropy, new networks and new governance in education. *Political Studies* 56 (4), 747–765.

Ball, S.J. (2009) Beyond networks? A brief response to 'which networks matter in education governance' *Political Studies* 57 (3), 688–691.

Ball, S.J. (2012) *Global Education Inc*. Abingdon: Routledge.

Ball, S.J., Maguire, M. and Braun, A., with Hoskins, K. and Perryman, J. (2012) *How Schools Do Policy*. Abingdon: Routledge.

Barber, M. (2001) High expectations and standards for all, no matter what. In: Fielding, M. (ed.) *Taking Education Really Seriously*. London: RoutledgeFalmer, 17–41.

Barber, M. (2007) *Instruction to Deliver*. London: Politico's Publishing.

Barker, B. (1999) Double vision: 40 years on. In: Tomlinson, H., Gunter, H. and Smith, P. (eds) *Living Headship: Voices, Values and Vision*. London: PCP, 73–85.

Barker, B. (2010) *The Pendulum Swings*. Stoke-on-Trent: Trentham Books.

Baron, G. and Taylor, W. (eds) (1969) *Educational Administration and the Social Sciences*. London: The Athlone Press.

Barta, T. (2007) On pain of extinction: laws of nature and history in Darwin, Marx and Arendt. In: King, R.H. and Stone, D. (eds) *Hannah Arendt and the Uses of History: Imperialism, Nation, Race, and Genocide*. New York: Berghahn Books, 87–105.

Baum, D., Bygrave, S. and Morton, S. (2011) Hannah Arendt 'After modernity'. *New Formations*. Number 71, Spring 2011, 6–13.

Beckett, F. (2007) *The Great City Academy Fraud*. London: Continuum.

Benhabib, S. (2000) *The Reluctant Modernism of Hannah Arendt*. Lanham, MD: Rowman and Littlefield Publishers Inc.

Benington, J. and Moore, M.H. (eds) (2011) *Public Value: Theory and Practice*. Basingstoke: Palgrave MacMillan.

Bennett, N., Crawford, M. and Riches, C. (eds) (1992) *Managing Change in Education*. London: PCP.

Bennett, N., Crawford, M. and Cartwright, M. (eds) (2003a) *Effective Educational Leadership*. London: PCP.

Bennett, N., Wise, C., Woods, P. and Harvey, J. (2003b) *Distributed Leadership*. Nottingham: NCSL.

Berkhout, S. (2007) Democratization and the remaking of teachers in South Africa. In: Butt, G. and Gunter, H.M. (eds) *Modernizing Schools*. London: Continuum, 149–162.

Bernstein, R.J. (1997) 'The banality of evil' reconsidered. In: Calhoun, C. and McGowan, J. (eds) *Hannah Arendt and the Meaning of Politics*. Minneapolis, MN: University of Minnesota, 297–322.

Bhabha, H.K. (1994) *The Location of Culture*. Abingdon: Routledge.

Biesta, G. (2010) How to exist politically and learn from it: Hannah Arendt and the problem of democratic education. *Teachers College Record* 112 (2), 556–575.

Blackmore, J. (1999) *Troubling Women, Feminism, Leadership and Educational Change*. Buckingham: OUP.

Blackmore, J. and Sachs, J. (2007) *Performing and Reforming Leaders: Gender, Educational Restructuring and Organizational Change*. Albany, NY: State University of New York Press.

Blair, T. (1998) *Speech to the New Heads Conference*. London: DfEE.

Blunkett, D. (2000) Blunkett sets out radical new agenda for inner city school diversity and improvement. 15 March 2000. London: DCSF. www.dcsf.gov.uk/pns/DisplayPN.cgi?pn_id=2000_0106 (accessed 2 October 2009).

Bobbitt, P. (2002) *The Shield of Achilles*. London: Penguin.

Boffey, D. (2012) Gove faces threat of legal action as rebel primary school battles his academy plan. *The Observer* 9 January 2012, 10.

Bogotch, I., Beachum, F., Blount, J., Brooks, J., English, F., with Jansen, J. (2008) *Radicalizing Educational Leadership*. Rotterdam: Sense Publishers.

Bourdieu, P. (1990) *In Other Words*. Cambridge: Polity Press.

Bowe, R. and Ball, S.J., with Gold, A. (1992) *Reforming Education and Changing Schools*. London: Routledge.

Bowring, F. (2011) *Hannah Arendt: A Critical Introduction*. London: Pluto Press.

Buraway, M. (1979) *Manufacturing Consent*. Chicago, IL: The University of Chicago Press.

Bush, T. (ed) (1989) *Managing Education: Theory and Practice*. Milton Keynes: OUP.

Bush, T. (2011) *Theories of Educational Leadership and Management*. Fourth edition. London: Sage.

Bush, T. and Bell, L. (2002) *The Principles and Practice of Educational Management*. London: PCP.

Bush, T. and Kogan, M. (1982) *Directors of Education*. London: Harper Collins Publishers.

Bush, T., Bell, L., Bolam, R., Glatter, R. and Ribbins, P. (eds) (1999) *Educational Management: Redefining Theory, Policy and Practice*. London: PCP.

Busher, H. and Harris, A., with Wise, C. (2000) *Subject Leadership and School Improvement*. London: PCP.

Butler, J. (2007) 'I merely belong to them'. *London Review of Books* 29 (9), 26–28. www.lrb.co.uk/v29/judith-butler/I-merely-belong-to-them (accessed 5 October 2011).

Butler, J. and Spivak, G.C. (2010) *Who Sings the Nation State?* London: Seagull Books.

Butt, G. and Gunter, H.M. (eds) (2007) *Modernizing Schools: People, Learning and Organizations.* London: Continuum.

Caldwell, B. and Spinks, J.M. (1988) *The Self Managing School.* Lewes: The Falmer Press.

Calhoun, C. and McGowan, J. (eds) (1997) *Hannah Arendt and the Meaning of Politics.* Minneapolis, MN: University of Minnesota.

Canovan, M. (1995) *Hannah Arendt: A Reinterpretation of Her Political Thought.* Cambridge: Cambridge University Press.

Canovan, M. (1998) Introduction. In: Arendt, H. (1958) *The Human Condition.* Second edition. Chicago: The University of Chicago Press.

Chakrabortty, A. (2012) *Economics has failed us: but where are the fresh voices?* http://www.guardian.co.uk/commentisfree/2012/apr/16/economics-has-failed-us-alternative-voices/ (accessed 2 May 2012).

Chaytor, R. (2006) Mum's agony as she finds tot, 2, underwater. *Mirror.* http://www.mirror.co.uk/news/top-stories/2006/03/22/mum-s-agony-as-she-finds-tot-2-under-water-115875-16846529/ (accessed 13 October 2011).

Clark, L. (2012) 5,000 underperforming head teachers are blighting England's primary schools, warns inspector. *MailOnline.* http://www.dailymail.co.uk/news/article-2096784/Underperforming-head-teachers-blighting-Englands-schools-says-Ofsted-chief-inspector.html (accessed 6 February 2012).

Clark, P. (1998) *Back from the Brink.* London: Metro Books.

Clarke, J. and Newman, J. (1997) *The Managerial State.* London: Sage.

Coffield, F. and Williamson, B. (2012) *From Exam Factories to Communities of Discovery.* London: Institute of Education.

Cohen, N. (2011) Lest we forget, the City still thrives on greed. *The Observer.* http://www.guardian.co.uk/commentisfree/2011/oct/09/city-of-london-business-greed (accessed 13 October 2011).

Coleman, M. (2001) Achievement against the odds: the female secondary head-teachers in England and Wales. *School Leadership and Management* 21 (1), 75–100.

Coleman, M. (2002) *Women as Headteachers: Striking the Balance.* Stoke-on-Trent: Trentham Books.

Coleman, M. (2004) *Gender and Headship in the Twenty-First Century.* Nottingham: NCSL.

Coleman, M. and Earley, P. (2005) *Leadership and Management in Education.* Oxford: Oxford University Press.

Coles, M.J. and Southworth, G. (eds) (2005) *Developing Leadership.* Maidenhead: OUP.

Compton, M. and Weiner, L. (2008) *The Global Assault on Teaching, Teachers, and their Unions.* New York: Palgrave MacMillan.

Connell, R. (2007) *Southern Theory.* Cambridge: Polity Press.

Courtney, S. (2011) *Lesbian, Gay and Bisexual (LGB) Identity and School Leadership: English LGB School Leaders' Perspectives.* Unpublished MA dissertation, School of Education, University of Manchester.

Cox, C.B. and Dyson, A.E. (1968) *Fight for Education*. London: The Critical Quarterly Society.

Crawford, M., Kydd, L. and Riches, C. (eds) (1997) *Leadership and Teams in Educational Management*. Buckingham: OUP.

Curtis, K. (2001) Multicultural education and Arendtian conservatism. In: Gordon, M. (ed.) *Hannah Arendt and Education*. Boulder, Co: Westview Press, 127–152.

Davies, B. (ed.) (2005) *The Essentials of School Management*. London: PCP.

Davies, B., Ellison, L., Osborne, A. and West-Burnham, J. (1990) *Education Management for the 1990s*. Harlow: Longman.

Davis, A. (2012) Gove: critics of academies are happy with failure. *Evening Standard*. 4 January 2012, 13.

Day, C., Sammons, P., Hopkins, D., Harris, A., Leithwood, K., Gu, Q., Brown, E., Ahtaridou, E. and Kington, A. (2009) *The Impact of School Leadership on Pupil Outcomes*. London: DCSF/NCSL.

Delanty, G. (1997) *Social Science: Beyond Constructivism and Realism*. Buckingham: Open University Press.

DfE (2010) The case for school freedom: national and international evidence (Gove mythbuster 2). http://www.education.gov.uk/news/news/freeschools (accessed 2 July 2010).

DfEE (1997) *Excellence in Schools*. London: DfEE. Cm 3681.

DfEE (1998) *Teachers: Meeting the Challenge of Change*. London: DfEE.

DfES (2004a) *Smoking Out Underachievement: Guidance and Advice to Help Secondary Schools Use Value Added Approaches with Data*. London: DfES.

DfES (2004b) *National Standards for Headteachers*. London: DfES.

DfES/PwC (2007) *Independent Study into School Leadership*. London: DfES.

Duarte, E. (2001) The eclipse of thinking: an Arendtian critique of cooperative learning. In: Gordon, M. (ed.) *Hannah Arendt and Education*. Boulder, Co: Westview Press, 201–223.

Duarte, E. (2009) In the time of thinking differently. *Philosophy of Education*, 250–252.

Duarte, E. (2010a) Educational thinking and the conservation of the revolutionary. *Teachers College Record* 112 (2), 488–508.

Duarte, E. (2010b) Becoming a subject of thinking: philosophers *in* education. *Philosophy of Education*, 262–265.

Elliott, J. (2011) The birth of Norwich's First School Academy: a case study. In: Gunter, H.M. (ed.) *The State and Education Policy: The Academies Programme*, 52–65.

Everard, K.B. and Morris, G. (1988) *Effective School Management*. London: PCP.

Fielding, M. (2006) Leadership, radical student engagement and the necessity of person-centred education. *International Journal of Leadership in Education* 9 (4), 299–313.

Fielding, M. and Moss, P. (2011) *Radical Education and the Common School*. Abingdon: Routledge.

Fitzgerald, T. (2007) Remodelling schools and schooling, teachers and teaching: a New Zealand perspective. In: Butt, G. and Gunter, H.M. (eds) *Modernizing Schools*. London: Continuum, 163–176.

Fitzgerald, T., White, J., and Gunter, H.M. (2012) *Hard Labour? Academic Work and the Changing Landscape of Higher Education*. Bingley: Emerald.

Forde, R., Hobby, R. and Lees, A. (2000) *The Lessons of Leadership*. London: Hay Management Consultants Ltd.

Foster, W. (1986) *Paradigms and Promises*. Amherst, NY: Prometheus Books.

Fraser, N. (2004) Hannah Arendt in the 21st Century. *Contemporary Political Theory* 3 (3), 253–261.

Fullan, M. (2003) *Change Forces with a Vengeance*. London: RoutledgeFalmer.

Furedi, F. (2006) *Culture of Fear Revisited*. London: Continuum.

Galton, M. (2007) New Labour and education: an evidence-based analysis. *Forum* 49 (1 and 2), 157–177.

Gamble, A. (2012) Have the social sciences failed us? http://www.britac.ac.uk/policyperspectives/have-the-social-sciences-failed-us.htm (accessed 2 May 2012).

Gandin, L.A. and Apple, M. (2003) Educating the state, democratizing knowledge: the citizen school project in Porte Alegre, Brazil. In: Apple, M.W., Aasen, P., Kim Cho, M., Gandin, L.A., Oliver, A., Sung, Y-K., Tavares, H, and Wong, T-H. (eds) *The State and the Politics of Knowledge*. New York: RoutledgeFalmer, 193–219.

Gewirtz, S. (2001) Cloning the Blairs: New Labour's programme for the re-socialization of working-class parents. *Journal of Education Policy* 16 (4), 365–378.

Gewirtz, S. (2002) *The Managerial School*. London: Routledge.

Gewirtz, S., Mahony, P., Hextall, I. and Cribb, I. (eds) (2009) *Changing Teacher Professionalism*. Abingdon: Routledge.

Giroux, H.A. (2011) Foreword: governing through crime and the pedagogy of punishment. In: Saltman, K.J. and Gabbard, D.A. (eds) *Education as Enforcement*. Second edition. New York, NY: Routledge, vii–xvi.

Giuliani, R.W. with Kurson, K. (2005) *Leadership*. London: Time Warner Paperbacks.

Glatter, R. (ed.) (1989) *Educational Institutions and their Environments*. Milton Keynes: OUP.

Goodwin, M. (2009) Which networks matter in education governance? A reply to Ball's 'New Philanthropy, New Networks and New Governance in Education'. *Political Studies* 57 (3), 680–687.

Gordon, M. (2001a) *Hannah Arendt and Education*. Boulder, Co.: Westview Press.

Gordon, M. (2001b) Introduction. In: Gordon, M. (ed.) *Hannah Arendt and Education*. Boulder, Co.: Westview Press, 1–9.

Gordon, M. (2001c) Hannah Arendt on authority: conservativism in education reconsidered. In: Gordon, M. (ed.) *Hannah Arendt and Education*. Boulder, Co.: Westview Press, 37–65.

Gove, M. (2010) Speech to the National College Annual Conference, 17th June 2010. http://www.michaelgove.com/content/national_college_annual_conference (accessed 29 September 2010).

Gove, M. (2012) Michael Gove speech on academies. www.education.gov.uk/inthenews/speeches/a00201425/michael-gove-speech-on-academies 5 January 2012 (accessed 12 January 2012).

Grace, G. (1995) *School Leadership: Beyond Educational Management*. London: The Falmer Press.

Greenfield, T. (1978) Where does self belong in the study of organisation? Response to a symposium. *Educational Administration* 6 (1), 81–101.

Greenfield, T. and Ribbins, P. (eds) (1993) *Greenfield on Educational Administration*. London: Routledge.

Gronn, P. (2003) *The New Work of Educational Leaders*. London: PCP.

Gronn, P. (2009) Hybrid leadership. In: Leithwood, K., Mascall, B. and Strauss, T. (eds) *Distributed Leadership According to the Evidence*. New York: Routledge, 17–40.

Gronn, P. (2010) Leadership: its genealogy, configuration and trajectory. *Journal of Educational Administration and History* 42 (4), 405–435.

Gunter, H.M. (1997) *Rethinking Education: The Consequences of Jurassic Management*. London: Cassell.

Gunter, H.M. (1999) *An Intellectual History of the Field of Educational Management from 1960*. Unpublished PhD thesis, Keele University.

Gunter, H.M. (2001a) *Leaders and Leadership in Education*. London: PCP.

Gunter, H.M. (2001b) Teacher appraisal research networks 1980–2000. *Educational Review* 53 (3), 241–250.

Gunter, H.M. (2004) Labels and labelling in the field of educational leadership. *Discourse* 25 (1), 21–42.

Gunter, H.M. (2005) *Leading Teachers*. London: Continuum.

Gunter, H.M. (2008) KPEL project interview data. Unpublished.

Gunter, H.M. (ed.) (2011) *The State and Education Policy: The Academies Programme*. London: Continuum.

Gunter, H.M. (2012a) *Leadership and Education Reform*. Bristol: The Policy Press.

Gunter, H.M. (2012b) Intellectual work and knowledge production. In: Fitzgerald, T., White, J. and Gunter, H.M. (eds) *Hard Labour? Academic Work and the Changing Landscape of Higher Education*. Bingley: Emerald.

Gunter, H.M. and Fitzgerald, T. (2011) The pendulum swings: but where? Part 1. *Journal of Educational Administration and History* 43 (4), 283–289.

Gunter, H.M. and Forrester, G. (2009) Education reform and school leadership. In: Brookes, S. and Grint, K. (eds) *The Public Sector Leadership Challenge*. London: Palgrave, 54–69.

Gunter, H.M. and Hall, D. (2013) Public trust and education. In: Llewellyn, S., Brookes, S. and Mahon, A. (eds) *Trust and Confidence in Government and Public Services*. London: Routledge, 204–220.

Gunter, H.M. and Thomson, P. (2006) Stories from the field of commissioned research. Paper presented to the British Educational Research Association Conference, University of Warwick, September 2006.

Gunter, H.M. and Thomson, P. (2009) The makeover: a new logic in leadership development in England? *Educational Review* 61 (4), 469–483.

Gunter, H.M. and Thomson, P. (2010) Life on Mars: headteachers before the National College. *Journal of Educational Administration and History* 42 (3), 203–222.

Gunter, H.M., Hall, D. and Bragg, J. (2013) Distributed leadership: a study in knowledge production. *Educational Leadership, Management and Administration.* In press.

Hailsham, Q. (1976) Elective dictatorship. *The Listener,* 21 October 1976, 496–500.

Hall, D., Gunter, H.M. and Bragg, J. (2011) *Distributed Leadership and the Social Practices of School Organisation in England Project* (RES-000–22-3610). Report to the ESRC.

Hall, D., Gunter, H.M., and Bragg, J. (2012) Leadership, New Public Management and the re-modeling and regulation of teacher identities. *International Journal of Leadership in Education.* In press.

Hall, D., Gunter, H.M. and Bragg, J. (2012) The strange case of the emergence of distributed leadership in schools in England. *Educational Review.* DOI: 10.1080/0013 1911.2012.718257.

Hall, V. (1996) *Dancing on the Ceiling.* London: PCP.

Hall, V. (1999) Gender and education management: duel or dialogue? In: Bush, T., Bell, L., Bolam, R., Glatter, R. and Ribbins, P. (eds) *Educational Management: Redefining Theory, Policy and Practice.* London: PCP, 155–165.

Hall, V. and Southworth, G. (1997) Headship. *School Leadership and Management* 17 (2), 151–169.

Hallinger, P. and Heck, R.H. (1996) Reassessing the principal's role in school effectiveness: a review of empirical research, 1980–1995. *Educational Administration Quarterly* 32 (1), 5–44.

Hargreaves, A. (2003) *Teaching in the Knowledge Society: Education in the Age of Insecurity.* New York, NY: Teachers College Press.

Hargreaves, D.H. and Hopkins, D. (1991) *The Empowered School.* London: Cassell.

Harris, A. and Bennett, N. (eds) (2001) *School Effectiveness and School Improvement.* London: Continuum.

Harris, A. and Lambert, L. (2003) *Building Leadership Capacity for School Improvement.* Maidenhead: Open University Press.

Harris, A., Bennett, N. and Preedy, M. (eds) (1997) *Organizational Effectiveness and Improvement in Education.* Buckingham: OUP.

Hartley, D. (2007) The emergence of distributed leadership in education: why now? *British Journal of Educational Studies* 55 (2), 202–214.

Harvey, D. (2007) *A Brief History of Neoliberalism.* Oxford: Oxford University Press.

Hatcher, R. (2011) Local government against local democracy: a case study of a bid for building schools for the future funding for an academy. In: Gunter, H.M. (ed.) *The State and Education Policy: The Academies Programme.* London: Continuum, 39–51.

Hatcher, R. (2012) Democracy and governance in the local school system. *Journal of Educational Administration and History* 44 (1), 21–42.

Hatcher, R. and Jones, K. (2006) Researching resistance: campaigns against academies in England. *British Journal of Educational Studies* 54 (3), 329–351.

Helsby, G. (1999) *Changing Teachers' Work*. Buckingham: OUP.

Higgins, C. (2010) Education, crisis, and the human condition: Arendt after 50 years. *Teachers College Record* 112 (2), 375–385.

Hind, D. (2010) *The Return of the Public*. London: Verso.

Hodgkinson, C. (1983) *The Philosophy of Leadership*. Oxford: Basil Blackwell.

Hollins, K., Gunter, H.M. and Thomson, P. (2006) Living Improvement: a case study of a secondary school in England. *Improving Schools* 9 (2), 141–152.

Honig, B. (1995) Introduction. In: Honig, B. (ed.) *Feminist Interpretations of Hannah Arendt*. University Park, PA: Pennsylvania State University Press.

Hood, C. (2007) A public management for all seasons? *Public Administration* 69, Spring, 3–29.

Hood, C. and Peters, G. (2004) The middle aging of new public management: into the age of paradox? *Journal of Public Administration Research and Theory* 14 (3), 267–282.

Hood, C., Rothstein, H., and Baldwin, R. (2004) *The Government of Risk*. Oxford: Oxford University Press.

Hopkins, D. (2001) *School Improvement For Real*. London: RoutledgeFalmer.

Hopkins, D. (2007) *Every School a Great School*. Maidenhead: OUP.

Howson, J. (2007) *Thirteenth Annual Report: The State of the Labour Market for Senior Staff in Schools in England and Wales 2006–2007*. London: Education Data Surveys at TSL Education Limited.

Howson, J. (2008) *Fourteenth Annual Report: The State of the Labour Market for Senior Staff in Schools in England and Wales 2007–2008*. London: Education Data Surveys at TSL Education Limited.

Hoyle, E. (1982) Micropolitics of educational organisations. *Educational Management and Administration* 10 (2), 87–98.

Hoyle, E. (1986) The management of schools: theory and practice. In Hoyle, E., and McMahon, A. (eds) *World Yearbook of Education 1986: The Management of Schools*. London: Kogan Page.

Hoyle, E. (1999) The two faces of micropolitics. *School Leadership and Management* 19 (2), 213–222.

Huber, S., Moorman, H. and Pont, B. (2007) *School Leadership for Systemic Improvement in England: A Case Study Report for the OECD Activity Improving School Leadership*. Paris: OECD.

Hughes, M. (1978) Education administration: pure or applied? Inaugural professorial lecture. Birmingham: University of Birmingham.

Hughes, M., Ribbins, P., and Thomas, H. (1985) *Managing Education: The System and the Institution*. Eastbourne: Holt, Rinehart and Winston.

Inglis, F. (2011) Economical with the actualité. *Times Higher Education*, 6 October 2011, 36–41.

Jalušič, V. (2007) Post-totalitarian elements and Eichmann's mentality in the Yugoslav war and mass killings. In: King, R.H. and Stone, D. (eds) *Hannah*

Arendt and the Uses of History: Imperialism, Nation, Race, and Genocide. New York: Berghahn Books, 147–170.

John, D. (1980) *Leadership in Schools*. London: Heinemann Educational Books.

Jordan, B. (2012) *Social Science and the Crisis*. The Policy Press E-Newsletter. Bristol: The Policy Press.

Judge, P. (2000) *Businessweek Online Daily Briefing*. March 2 2000. http://www.greenstar.org/butterflies/Hole-in-the-Wall.htm (accessed 27 July 2012).

Judt, T. (2010) *Ill Fares the Land*. New York: Penguin Press.

King, R.H. (2007) Arendt between past and future. In: King, R.H. and Stone, D. (eds) *Hannah Arendt and the Uses of History: Imperialism, Nation, Race, and Genocide*. New York: Berghahn Books, 250–261.

King, R.H. (2011) Hannah Arendt and the concept of revolution in the 1960s. *New Formations*. Number 71, Spring 2011, 30–45.

King, R.H. and Stone, D. (2008) Introduction. In: King, R.H. and Stone, D. (eds) *Hannah Arendt and the Uses of History: Imperialism, Nation, Race, and Genocide*. New York: Berghahn Books, 1–17.

Kirsch, A. (2009) Beware of pity: Arendt and the power of the impersonal. http://www.newyorker.com/online/blogs/newsdesk/2009/09/jane-mayer-calling-hannah-arendt.html (accessed 24 October 2011).

Knight, B. (1989) *Managing School Time*. Harlow: Longman.

Kohn, J. (1994) Introduction. In: Arendt, H. *Essays in Understanding, 1930–1954: Formation, Exile and Totalitarianism*. New York, NY: Schocken Books.

Kohn, J. (2003) Introduction. In: Arendt, H. *Responsibility and Judgement*. New York, NY: Schocken Books.

Kohn, J. (2006) Introduction. In: Arendt, H. *Between Past and Future*. New York, NY: Penguin Books.

Kydd, L., Anderson, L. and Newton, W. (eds) (2003) *Leading People and Teams in Education*. London: PCP.

Lane, A. (2001) Is Hannah Arendt a multiculturalist? In: Gordon, M. (ed.) *Hannah Arendt and Education*. Boulder, Co.: Westview Press, 153–173.

Law, S. and Glover, D. (2000) *Educational Leadership and Learning*. Buckingham: OUP.

Le Grand, J. and Bartlett, W. (eds) (1993) *Quasi-markets and Social Policy*. London: Macmillan.

Leithwood, K., Day, C., Sammons, P., Harris, A. and Hopkins, D. (2006) *Seven Strong Claims About Successful School Leadership*. Nottingham: NCSL.

Leithwood, K., Jantzi, D. and Steinbach, R. (1999) *Changing Leadership for Changing Times*. Buckingham: OUP.

Leo, E., Galloway, D. and Hearne, P. (2010) *Academies and Educational Reform: Governance, Leadership and Strategy*. Bristol: Multilingual Matters.

Lepkowska, D. (2012) 'What did I do wrong?' *The Guardian* 12th June 2012, p34.

Levacic, R. (ed.) (1989) *Financial Management in Education*. Milton Keynes: OUP.

Levinson, N. (2001) The paradox of natality: teaching in the midst of belatedness. In: Gordon, M. (ed.) *Hannah Arendt and Education*. Boulder, Co.: Westview Press, 11–36.

Levinson, N. (2002) 'But some people will not': Arendtian interventions in education. *Philosophy of Education*, 200–208.

Levinson, N. (2010) A 'more general crisis': Hannah Arendt, world-alienation, and the challenges of teaching for the world as it is. *Teachers College Record* 112 (2), 464–487.

Lingard, B., Hayes, D., Mills, M. and Christie, P. (2003) *Leading Learning.* Maidenhead: OUP.

Lloyd, S. (2005) *Distributed Leadership: The Rhetoric and the Reality.* Nottingham: NCSL.

Lortie, D.C. (2009) *School Principal.* Chicago, IL: The Chicago University Press.

Lumby, J. and Coleman, M. (2007) *Leadership and Diversity: Challenging Theory and Practice in Education.* London: Sage.

MacBeath, J., Oduro, G.K.T. and Waterhouse, J. (2004) *Distributed Leadership in Action: Full Report.* Nottingham: NCSL.

McCann, L. (2012) Treated like imbeciles. http://www.socialsciencespace.com/2012/05/treated-like-imbeciles (accessed 31 May 2012).

McGinity, R. and Gunter, H.M. (2012) Living improvement 2: a case study of a secondary school in England. *Improving Schools* 15 (3), 228–244.

McLaughlin, K., Osborne, S. and Ferlie, E. (2002) *New Public Management: Current Trends and Future Prospects.* London: Routledge.

McNamara, O., Howson, J., Gunter, H.M. and Fryers, A. (2009) *The Leadership Aspirations and Careers of Black and Ethnic Minority Teachers.* Birmingham: NASUWT.

McNamara, O., Howson, J., Gunter, H.M. and Fryers, A. (2010) *No Job For a Woman: The Impact of Gender in School Leadership.* Birmingham: NASUWT.

McNamara, O., Howson, J., Gunter, H.M., Sprigade, A. and Onat-Stelmas, Z. (2008) *Women Teachers' Careers.* Birmingham: NASUWT.

Marland, M. (ed.) (1986) *School Management Skills.* London: Heinemann Educational Books.

Marquand, D. (2004) *Decline of the Public.* Cambridge: Polity Press.

Marshall, C. (2000) The emperor and research on women in school leadership: a response to Julie Laible's loving epistemology. *Qualitative Studies in Education* 13 (6), 699–704.

Mayer, J. (2009) Jane Mayer calling Hannah Arendt. http://www.newyorker.com/online/blogs/newsdesk/2009/09/jane-mayer-calling-hannah-arendt.html (accessed 24 October 2011).

Miller, J. (1995) Thinking without a banister. *London Review of Books.* 17 (20), 34–35. www.lrb.co.uk/v17/n20/james-miller/thinking-without-a-banister (accessed 5 October 2011).

Moorhead, J. (2012) Head-hunting. *The Guardian*, 21 February 2012, 32.

Moran, M. (2007) *The British Regulatory State.* Oxford: Oxford University Press.

Morrison, M. (2009) *Leadership and Learning.* Charlotte, NC: IAP.

Munby, S. (2006) *The School Leadership Challenges for the 21st Century.* Nottingham: NCSL.

Newman, J. and Clarke, J. (2009) *Publics, Politics and Power.* London: Sage.

Niesche, R. (2012) Working against the grain. *Discourse: Studies in the Cultural Politics of Education*. Online first.

Northern, S. (2011) Follow my (associate senior) leader. *The Guardian*, 15 November 2011.

O'Brien, M. (1981) *The Politics of Reproduction*. London: Routledge and Kegan Paul.

O'Reilly, D. and Reed, M. (2010) 'Leaderism': an evolution of managerialism in UK public service reform. *Public Administration* 88 (4), 960–978.

Ouston, J. (ed.) (1993) *Women in Educational Management*. Harlow: Longman.

Owens, P. (2011) The supreme social concept: the un-worldliness of modern security. *New Formations*. Number 71, Spring 2011, 14–29.

Ozga, J. (1987) Studying education policy through the lives of the policymakers: an attempt to close the macro-micro gap. In Walker, S. and Barton, L. (eds) *Changing Policies, Changing Teachers: New Directions for Schooling?* Milton Keynes: OUP.

Ozga, J. (2000a) *Policy Research in Educational Settings*. Buckingham: OUP.

Ozga, J. (2000b) Leadership in education: the problem, not the solution? *Discourse: Studies in the Cultural Politics of Education* 21 (3), 355–361.

Ozga, J. (2009) Governing education through data in England: from regulation to self-evaluation. *Journal of Education Policy* 24 (2), 149–162.

Page, D. (2011) From principled dissent to cognitive escape: managerial resistance in the English further education sector. *Journal of Vocational Education and Training* 63 (1), 1–13.

Pitkin, H.F. (1998) *The Attack of the Blob: Hannah Arendt's Concept of the Social*. Chicago, IL: The University of Chicago Press.

Pollitt, C. (1990) *Managerialism and the Public Services: The Anglo-American Experience*. Oxford: Blackwell.

Pollitt, C. (2007) New Labour's re-disorganisation. *Public Management Review* 9 (4), 529–543.

Power, M. (1999) *The Audit Society*. Oxford: Oxford University Press.

Preedy, M., Bennett, N. and Wise, C. (eds) (2012) *Educational Leadership: Context, Strategy and Collaboration*. Milton Keynes: OUP.

Preedy, M., Glatter, R. and Levacic, R. (eds) (1997) *Educational Management: Strategy, Quality and Resources*. Buckingham: OUP.

Preedy, M., Glatter, R. and Wise, C. (eds) (2003) *Strategic Leadership and Educational Improvement*. London: PCP.

PricewaterhouseCoopers (2008) *Academies Evaluation: Fifth Annual Report*. London: DCSF.

Raffo, C., Dyson, A., Gunter, H.M, Hall, D., Jones, L. and Kalambouka, A. (eds) (2010) *Education and Poverty in Affluent Countries*. London: Routledge.

Ranson, S. (1993) Markets or democracy for education. *British Journal of Educational Studies* 41 (4), 333–352.

Ranson, S. (1995) Theorising education policy. *Journal of Education Policy* 10 (4), 427–448.

Ranson, S. (2000) Recognizing the pedagogy of voice in a learning community. *Education Management and Administration* 28 (3), 263–279.

Ravitch, D. (2010a) *The Death and Life of the Great American School System.* New York: Basic Books.

Ravitch, D. (2010b) The myth of charter schools. *The New York Review of Books*, 11 November 2010. http://www.nybooks.com/articles/archives/2010/nov/11/myth-charter-schools/ (accessed 26 January 2011).

Reay, D., and William, D. (1999) 'I'll be a nothing': structure, agency and the construction of identity through assessment, *British Educational Research Journal* 25(3), 343–354.

Reay, D., David, M.E. and Ball, S.J. (2005) *Degrees of Choice: Social Class, Race and Gender in Higher Education.* Stoke-on-Trent: Trentham Books.

Reynolds, D., Sammons, P., Stoll, L., Barber, M. and Hillman, J. (1996) School effectiveness and school improvement in the United Kingdom. *School Effectiveness and School Improvement* 7 (2), 133–158.

Ribbins, P. (ed.) (1997) *Leaders and Leadership in the School, College and University.* London: Cassell.

Ribbins, P. (2008) A life and career based framework for the study of leaders in education: problems, possibilities and prescriptions. In: Crow, G., Lumby, J. and Pashiardies, P. (eds) *International Handbook on the Preparation and Development of School Leaders.* London: Routeldge, 61–80.

Rich, A. (1979) *On Lies, Secrets and Silence: Selected Prose, 1966–1978.* New York: Norton.

Richardson, E. (1973) *The Teacher, the School and the Task of Management.* London: Heinemann.

Richardson, H. (2012) Dock truants' child benefit, ministers urged. http://www.bbc.co.uk/news/education-17705238 (accessed 11 July 2012).

Riches, C. and Morgan, C. (eds) (1989) *Human Resource Management.* Milton Keynes: OUP.

Rizvi, F. and Lingard, B. (2010) *Globalizing Education Policy.* London: Routledge.

Robin, C. (2007) Dragon-slayers. *London Review of Books* 29 (1), 18–20. www.lrb.co.uk/v29/n01/corey-robin/dragon-slayers (accessed 5 October 2011).

Saint-Martin, D. (2000) *Building the New Managerialist State.* Oxford: Oxford University Press.

Saltman, K.J. and Gabbard, D.A. (2011) *Education as Enforcement.* Second edition. New York, NY: Routledge.

Samier, E. (2008) The problem of passive evil in educational administration: moral implications of doing nothing. *International Studies in Educational Administration* 36 (1), 2–21.

Sammons, P., Thomas, S. and Mortimore, P. (1997) *Forging Links: Effective Schools and Effective Departments.* London: PCP.

Sandler, M.R. (2010) *Social Entrepreneurship in Education.* Lanthan, MA: Bowman and Littlefield Education.

Schell, J. (2006) Introduction: the Arendtian revolutions. In: Arendt, H. *On Revolution.* New York, NY: Penguin Books.

Scott, J.C. (1998) *Seeing Like a State.* New Haven: Yale University Press.

Sennett, R. (1999) *The Corrosion of Character*. New York, NY: W.W. Norton & Company.

Sennett, R. (2002) *The Fall of Public Man*. London: Penguin.

Sennett, R. (2012) *Together: The Rituals, Pleasures and Politics of Cooperation*. London: Allen Lane.

Slee, R. and Weiner, G., with Tomlinson, S. (eds) (1998) *School Effectiveness for Whom? Challenges to the School Effectiveness and School Improvement Movements*. London: Falmer Press.

Smyth, J. (ed.) (1989) *Critical Perspectives on Educational Leadership*. London: Falmer Press.

Smyth, J. (ed.) (1993) *A Socially Critical View of the Self Managing School*. London: The Falmer Press.

Smyth, J. (2006) Educational leadership that fosters 'student voice'. *International Journal of Leadership in Education* 9 (4), 279–284.

Smyth, J. (2011) *Critical Pedagogy for Social Justice*. London: Continuum.

Smyth, J. and McInerney, P. (2007) *Teachers in the Middle*. New York, NY: Peter Lang.

Smyth, J., Angus, L., Down, B. and Mcinerney, P. (2008) *Critically Engaged Learning*. New York, NY: Peter Lang.

Smyth, J. and Hattam, R., with Cannon, J., Edwards, J., Wilson, N. and Wurst, S. (2004) *Dropping Out, Drifting Off, Being Excluded*. New York, NY: Peter Lang.

Southworth, G.W. (1995) *Looking into Primary Headship*. London: Falmer Press.

Sprigade, A. and Howson, J. (2011) *Seventeenth Annual Report: The State of the Labour Market for Senior Staff in Schools in England and Wales, 2010–2011*. London: Education Data Surveys.

Squires, P. (ed.) (2008) *Asbo Nation*. Bristol: Policy Press.

Stone, D. (2011) Defending the plural: Hannah Arendt and genocide studies. *New Formations*. Number 71, Spring 2011, 46–57.

Strathern, M. (2000) The tyranny of transparency. *British Educational Research Journal* 26 (3), 309–321.

Strong, T. (2012) *Politics Without Vision: Thinking Without a Banister in the Twentieth Century*. Chicago, IL: The University of Chicago Press.

Stubbs, M. (2003) *A Head of the Class*. London: John Murray.

Swift, S. (2011) Hannah Arendt's tactlessness: reading Eichmann in Jerusalem. *New Formations*. Number 71, Spring 2011, 79–94.

Tamboukou, M. (2010) Narratives from within: an Arendtian approach to life histories and the writing of history. *Journal of Educational Administration and History*, 42 (2), 115–131.

Tamboukou, M. (2012) Truth telling in Foucault and Arendt: parrhesia, the pariah and academics in dark times. *Journal of Education Policy*. Online first.

Taysum, A. and Gunter, H.M. (2008) A critical approach to researching social justice and school leadership in England. *Education, Citizenship and Social Justice* 3 (2), 211–227.

The Independent (2006) Angry last words of a dying man. *The Independent.* http://www.independent.co.uk/news/uk/crime/angry-last-words-of-a-dying-man-425765.html (accessed 13 October 2011).

Thomas, H., Butt, G., Fielding, A., Foster, J., Gunter, H.M., Lance, A., Pilkington, R., Potts, E., Powers, S., Rayner, S., Rutherford, D., Selwood, I. and Szwed, C. (2004) *The Evaluation of the Transforming the School Workforce Pathfinder Project. Research Report 541.* London: DfES.

Thomson, P. (2009) *School Leadership: Heads on the Block?* London: Routledge.

Thomson, P. (2010) A critical pedagogy of global place: regeneration in and as action. In: Raffo, C., Dyson, A., Gunter, H., Hall, D., Jones, L. and Kalambouka, A. (eds) *Education and Poverty in Affluent Countries.* New York: Routledge, 124–134.

Thomson, P. and Gunter, H.M. (2006) From 'consulting pupils' to 'pupils as researchers': a situated case narrative. *British Educational Research Journal* 32 (6), 839–856.

Thrupp, M. and Willmott, R. (2003) *Education Management in Managerialist Times.* Maidenhead: OUP.

Tooley, J. (1995) Markets or democracy for education? A reply to Stewart Ranson. *British Journal of Educational Studies* 43 (1), 21–34.

Troman, G. and Woods, P. (2001) *Primary Teachers' Stress.* London: Routledge.

Wacquant, L. (2009) *Punishing the Poor.* Durham, NC: Duke University Press.

Wallace, M. (2001) Sharing leadership of schools through teamwork: a justifiable risk? *Educational Management, Administration and Leadership* 29 (2), 153–167.

Watson, D. (1992) *Arendt.* London: Fontana Press.

Whitty, G., Power, S. and Halpin, D. (1998) *Devolution and Choice in Education.* Buckingham: OUP.

Wilby, P. (2012) Does Gove realise he is empowering future dictators? http://www.guardian.co.uk/education/2012/jan/30/gove-powers-total-schools-academies (accessed 3 February 2012).

Wilkinson, J. and Pickett, K. (2009) *The Spirit Level.* London: Penguin Books Ltd.

Winerip, M. (2012) Move to outsource teaching licensing process draws protest. *The New York Times.* http://www.nytimes.com/2012/05/07/education/new-procedure-for-t. . .tml?_r=1&pagewanted=all&src=ISMR_AP_LO_MST_FB&pagewanted=print (accessed 16 May 2012).

Winkley, D. (2002) *Handsworth Revolution.* London: Giles de la Mare Publishers Ltd.

Woods, P.A. (2005) *Democratic Leadership in Education.* London: PCP.

Woods, P., Woods, G. and Gunter, H.M. (2007) Academy schools and entrepreneurialism in education. *Journal of Education Policy* 22 (2), 263–285.

Wright, N. (2003) Principled 'bastard' leadership? A rejoinder to Gold, Evans, Earley, Halpin and Collarbone. *Educational Management and Administration* 31 (2), 139–143.

Wrigley, T. (2012) Achievement, poverty and privatisation in England: policy and evidence. *Improving Schools* 15 (1), 5–9.

Wrigley, T., Thomson, P. and Lingard, B. (eds) (2012a) *Changing Schools: Alternative Ways to Make a World of Difference*. Abingdon: Routledge.

Wrigley, T., Thomson, P. and Lingard, B. (2012b) Resources for changing schools. In: Wrigley, T., Thomson, P. and Lingard, B. (eds) *Changing Schools: Alternative Ways to Make a World of Difference*. Abingdon: Routledge, 194–214.

Yarker, P. (2005) On not being a teacher: the professional and personal costs of workforce remodelling. *Forum* 47 (2 and 3), 169–174.

Young, M. (2008) *Bringing Knowledge Back In*. Abingdon: Routledge.

Young-Bruehl, E. (1982) *Hannah Arendt: For Love of the World*. New Haven: Yale University Press.

Young-Bruehl, E. (2006) *Why Arendt Matters*. New Haven: Yale University Press.

Young-Bruehl, E. and Kohn, J. (2001) What and how we learned from Hannah Arendt: an exchange of letters. In: Gordon, M. (ed.) *Hannah Arendt and Education*. Boulder, Co.: Westview Press, 225–256.

Index

Hallinger 32
Hargreaves, A. 93
Hargreaves, D.H. 78, 107
Harris 78, 107
Hartley 92
Hatcher 36, 61
Helsby 95
Higgins 43, 126
Hind 111
Hodgkinson 30
Hood 54, 60, 76
Hopkins37, 78, 89, 107, 111
Honig 109, 126
Howson 106
Hoyle 26, 79
Huber 89
Hughes 24, 107

Inglis 58

Jalušič 41, 60
John 107
Jordan 18
Judge 114–115
Judt 39–4

King 4, 8, 47, 112, 117, 126
Kirsch 11
Knight 107
knowledge production 2, 5, 12, 14,
  18–19, 23–25, 37–38, 61, 87,
  104–105, 107–108, 116
Knowledge Production in Educational
  Leadership (KPEL) project 25–27,
  63, 67, 70
Kohn 4, 8, 9–11, 13, 46, 72, 81–82
Kydd 107

Lane 45
Law 107
leadership: children 4, 6, 19, 22, 24,
  27–29, 32–45, 54, 56, 59, 64–79,
  85–88, 91, 94–95, 101, 107–108,
  113–118, 122; distributed 81–102;
  gender 105–109; industry vii, 24, 89;
  New Public Management/Leadership
  54, 91, 92; roles in school 17, 23–24,
  29, 31–32, 36, 38–40, 42, 45, 54–71,
  77–101, 106, 114–118, 122; training

21, 24, 42, 56, 57, 60, 67, 72, 78, 97,
  114–11; transformational 23, 38, 57,
  68–69, 76, 89–90, 105, 113, 117;
  Transnational Leadership Package
  (TLP) 19, 21, 24–30, 36–37, 40–41,
  53, 59–60, 63, 75, 78, 88, 103–104,
  107, 109, 111–112, 116–122
Le Grand 92
Leithwood 22, 25, 32, 57, 93–94
Leo 25
Lepkowska 100
Levacic 107
Levinson 19, 43, 45, 118
Lingard 22, 26
Lloyd 89
Lortie 21
Lumby 107
Luxemborg 55

MacBeath 89
Marland 107
Marquand 76
Marshall 106
Mayer 8–9
McCann 18
McGinity 71
McLaughlin 92
McNamara 106
Miller 1, 2, 30
Moran 18, 117
Morrison 26
Moorhead 77
Munby 89

neoconservatism xii, 17, 22–23, 29, 35,
  39, 44, 54–55, 59, 62, 75, 82, 87–88,
  93, 101, 104–105, 110–113, 115, 117
neoliberalism ix, xii, 4, 17, 22–24, 27,
  29, 34–35, 39, 44, 54–55, 59, 62,
  75, 82, 87–88, 93, 101, 104–105,
  110–113, 115–117
neo–Marxism: ix
Newman 34, 92
Niesche 122
Northern 31

O'Brien 109
O'Reilly 93
Ouston 107